# READING ARISTOTLE'S *ETHICS*

# READING ARISTOTLE'S *ETHICS*
## *Virtue, Rhetoric, and Political Philosophy*

Aristide Tessitore

STATE UNIVERSITY OF NEW YORK PRESS

Published by
State University of New York Press, Albany

For information, address State University of New York Press,
State University Plaza, Albany, N.Y., 12246

Production by Dana Foote
Marketing by Fran Keneston

**Library of Congress Cataloging-in-Publication Data**

Tessitore, Aristide.
    Reading Aristotle's Ethics : virtue, rhetoric, and political
philosophy / Aristide Tessitore.
        p.   cm.
    Includes bibliographical references (p.   ) and index.
    ISBN 0–7914–3047–2 (hardcover : alk. paper). — ISBN 0–7914–3048–0
(pbk. : alk. paper)
        1. Aristotle. Nicomachean ethics.   2. Ethics, Ancient.
3. Virtue.   4. Political science—Philosophy.   5. Rhetoric, Ancient.
6. Aristotle—Ethics.   I. Title.
B430.T47   1996
171'.3—dc20                                                     96–12731
                                                                    CIP

10 9 8 7 6 5 4 3 2 1

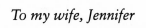

*To my wife, Jennifer*

# CONTENTS

# ACKNOWLEDGMENTS

This book developed over a long time and with the help of many people. First, I would like to thank my teachers and, in a special way, Christopher Bruell, Robert Faulkner, and Ernest Fortin, who patiently and thoughtfully monitored the fledgling version of this study in the form of a doctoral dissertation, and whose superb teaching conveyed the substantive basis for the enterprise as a whole. I have also benefited from many exchanges with friends and colleagues that have directly and indirectly contributed to the final product. In particular, I thank Larry Arnhart, Ronna Burger, Mary Nichols, Paul Rahe, Stephen Salkever, and Arlene Saxonhouse for generous and constructive evaluations of different aspects of the current manuscript, as well as Tony Preus and other reviewers at State University of New York Press for their instructive criticism. I have also learned much of importance about Aristotle from conversations with Timothy Burns, Daniel Cullen, Michael Pakaluk, and Catherine Zuckert. Congenial and inspiring colleagues at both Assumption College and Furman University have afforded me the very best of conditions for bringing this project to completion. The enthusiasm and dedication of several students has helped with both the clarification of ideas and the material assembly of the book. I am especially grateful for the assistance of Matthew Baughman, Andrew Matthews, and Alexander Stubb. Many friends have provided indispensable support over the years. Among them, I thank Edgar Bourque, Sharon and Devin Brown, Patrick Corrigan, John Franck, Mark Kilstofte, Daniel Mahoney, Leslie Rubin, Leonard Sorenson, Alexander Stubb, and Pamela Werrbach. My family has also offered constant and appreciated support throughout the entire project and beyond. The greatest source of encouragement has come from my wife, Jennifer, who has painstakingly edited the entire manuscript and provided daily inspiration in ways that exceed my capacity to acknowledge.

Even thinking requires a certain amount of external equipment as Aristotle might say, or, as he does say: *dianoia d'autē outhen kinei.* Generous support from the Earhart Foundation during the summers of 1993–94 made it possible to move this manuscript into print. I gratefully acknowledge their assistance, without which the project would still exist primarily in the realm of thought. I also thank the Duke Endowment and the Knight Foundation for their generous assistance in the form of Furman University Research and Professional Growth grants during 1993 and 1994.

Earlier versions of different parts of this book have been published elsewhere. Part of chapter 3 appeared as "A Political Reading of Aristotle's Treatment of Pleasure in the *Nicomachean Ethics*," *Political Theory* 17, no. 2 (May 1989): 247–65; and different sections of chapter 5 have appeared as "Making the City Safe for Philosophy, *Nicomachean Ethics*, Book 10," *American Political Science Review* 84, no. 4 (December 1990): 1251–62 and "Aristotle's Ambiguous Account of the Best Life," *Polity* 25, no. 2 (Winter 1992): 197–215. Permission to reprint revised portions of these articles is gratefully acknowledged.

# ABBREVIATIONS

| | |
|---|---|
| *Apology* | *Apo.* |
| *Eudemian Ethics* | *EE* |
| *Gorgias* | *Grg.* |
| *Magna Moralia* | *MM* |
| *Metaphysics* | *Meta.* |
| *Nicomachean Ethics* | *NE* |
| *Politics* | *Pol.* |
| *Posterior Analytics* | *Pos. An.* |
| *Protagoras* | *Protag.* |
| *Republic* | *Rep.* |
| *Rhetoric* | *Rh.* |
| *Topics* | *Top.* |

# Introduction

> He who thinks out everything for himself is best of all. Good also he who is persuaded by one who speaks well. But he who neither thinks for himself nor takes to heart what he hears from another is a useless man.
>
> —Hesiod, *Works and Days* 293–97
> *Nicomachean Ethics* 1.4.1095b10–13

There has been a remarkable resurgence of interest in Aristotle's moral and political philosophy during the last decade. More remarkable still, this renaissance is not limited to a single school of thought but has arisen simultaneously within a number of different disciplines and from a number of different perspectives within those disciplines. Despite the quantity and quality of much of this literature, it is not, however, entirely free from an unaristotelian partition among disciplines characteristic of modern scholarship. Studies of Aristotle's ethics, although often excellent, typically lack a deep appreciation for the political dimension within which that teaching is presented. Conversely, some of the best work on Aristotle's political teaching focuses almost exclusively on the *Politics* to the neglect of his ethical treatises. While there is a legitimate need for this kind of specialization, there also exists a need for studies that bring to light the unique way in which Aristotle integrates these two aspects of his understanding.

The problem is especially acute in the *Nicomachean Ethics*, which begins with the assertion that the study of ethics is part of the larger study of politics. *Reading Aristotle's Ethics* is intended to contribute to an appreciation for the seamless character of Aristotle's political thought by presenting the *Nicomachean Ethics*, as does Aristotle, as a work of political philosophy. It is distinctive in its attentiveness to the interplay between the political concerns that guide the practical aim of this book and the underlying philosophic perspective that is disclosed to its most attentive readers.

1

## CIVIC VIRTUE AND PHILOSOPHY

The conclusion of the *Nicomachean Ethics* is well known not only among students of philosophy but, more broadly, by virtually all who consider themselves to be students of Western culture: Complete or perfect happiness is to be found in the philosophic activity of contemplation, the practice of ethical virtue is happy in a secondary degree (10.7.1177a12–18, 10.8.1178a 9–10).[1] It may be that the success of the argument in the *Ethics* as a whole has obscured both the force of this jarring conclusion and the full measure of Aristotle's accomplishment. To the extent that the *Ethics* has become one of the classic texts of the Western tradition, it has succeeded in eliciting an acknowledgment on the part of nonphilosophers of the dignity and importance of the philosophic life.

That this was no easy task is suggested by recalling the animosity directed against philosophers (especially political philosophers) expressed in writings that antedate the *Ethics*. The suspect character of philosophy as it was perceived by the most spirited and ambitious contemporaries of Socrates is reflected in the plays of Aristophanes and the dialogues of Plato. In the *Clouds*, Aristophanes warns fellow citizens about the dangerously corrosive effect of philosophy on healthy political life. Socrates is pictured as an unwittingly malicious buffoon who, from the lofty vantage point of thought, debunks the gods who protect the city and uphold its laws. The most foolish act of the desperate Strepsiades turns out to be his decision to bring his son, Pheidippides, to study the art of argumentation with Socrates. As a result, Pheidippides loses respect for his father and, more generally, for the conventions that govern relations between parents and children. Aristophanes' comic depiction of Socratic philosophy suggests that Socrates is engaged in an enterprise the effects of which loosen the sacred ties that bind an individual to both family and fatherland.

An awareness of the politically dangerous effects of philosophic study is also preserved in the dialogues of Plato. One need only recall Callicles' stinging description of the politically incapacitating consequences of a serious preoccupation with philosophy or the vehemence of Anytus's response to Socrates' implicit criticism of great Athenian statesmen. Callicles, while acknowledging that some philosophic training is useful for the young, expresses disdain for the unmanly innocence and political vulnerability that results from prolonged involvement with such study. Preoccupation with the subtleties of speech forecloses the kind of noble action and high reputation characteristic of those who take an active part in political affairs (*Grg.* 484c–486d).[2] In speaking with Anytus, Socrates observes that several of the most celebrated Athenian statesmen were unable to teach political virtue to their sons. Anytus is outraged by what he perceives to be slander directed against those most responsible for Athenian greatness (*Meno* 92c–95a). His thinly veiled threat foreshadows the part he will play in bringing Socrates before the tribunal of the city for undermining the sacred and civic attachments of the most promising young Athenians.

It is, of course, in the trial and execution of Socrates that the hostility between the city and the philosopher reaches its dramatic climax. Moreover, Plato's presentation of Socrates' trial suggests that this animosity is in some sense reciprocal. Socratic criticism of Athenian justice is apparent in Socrates' transparently hubristic refusal to ask for mercy (*Apo.* 34b–35d) and subsequent argument that the only appropriate response for having lived as a philosopher would be for the city to accord him the honors reserved to Olympic heroes (*Apo.* 36b–37a). Even more telling because of its seeming universality, Socrates asserts that it is impossible for him or anyone seriously concerned with justice to survive in the political arena; a serious preoccupation with justice makes necessary a private rather than public life (*Apo.* 31d–32e).[3]

I recall these well-known facts regarding the problematic relationship between political philosophy and the city because it is against this backdrop that an often overlooked or underappreciated feature of Aristotle's political writing comes most fully into view. Although Aristotle, like his teacher before him, maintains the superiority of the philosophic life, his political treatises contain nothing like this overt warfare between philosophy and the city or, more precisely, between philosophers and citizens. Aristotle chooses rather to mute the conflict between philosophers and those who are primarily concerned about and responsible for the good of the city. This does not mean, however, that he denies the existence of a fundamental tension between the requirements of philosophic inquiry and the necessities that govern citizenship but, as I will attempt to demonstrate, that he combines his presentation of this problem with a persistent solicitude for the political concerns of his nonphilosophic readers. By adopting this approach, Aristotle succeeds in making the philosophic life more palatable to educated nonphilosophers, especially those who are primarily interested in civic virtue.

## THE RHETORICAL DIMENSION OF ETHICAL DISCOURSE

Traditional readings of the *Ethics* have assumed that, however problematic, the text in its present form is a relatively straightforward treatise or compilation of lecture notes, one that eschews rhetorical usage. I take issue with this view by suggesting that Aristotle's study is built upon a rhetorical framework that becomes visible when the question of its intended audience is raised with sufficient care. Some of the enduring problems generally believed to afflict the text are intelligible in light of the *rhetorical design* of the book as a whole. In using this expression I refer to a specifically Aristotelian understanding of rhetoric, one that requires further clarification.

The practice of rhetoric was criticized by Aristophanes as politically dangerous (esp. *Clouds* 112–15; 1071–82) and by Plato as a kind of "knack" contributing to the corruption of the soul through flattery (*Grg.* 462b–65e).[4] Like Aristophanes and Plato, Aristotle is also critical of the sophistic use of rhetoric; but, unlike them, he emphasizes the respectability of rhetoric itself by distinguishing it from and subordinating it to the study of politics (cf. *NE* 10.9.1181a13–18 and *Rh.* 1.2.1356a25–30). Aristotle maintains that rhetoric is an "art" that seeks to understand the various means of persuasion (*Rh.* 1.2.1355b27–35). Whereas the fundamental coherence and practical aim of Aristotle's study of rhetoric has recently received excellent consideration in the work of Arnhart, Lord, and Nichols,[5] these authors emphasize the oral character of rhetorical practice before the jurist and public assembly. Public discourse among citizens is unquestionably the primary, but not necessarily exclusive sphere of rhetorical influence. The very ambiguity of the Greek word for discourse (*logos*) points to another possible use of rhetoric—not only in the spoken word but also in the written one and, most deeply, in the very manner of conceiving and presenting a particular point or teaching. Indeed, Aristotle suggests this more general usage when he asserts that everyone practices rhetoric (and dialectic) to some extent at least, since everyone finds it necessary to criticize or to defend an argument (*logos*) (*Rh.* 1.1.1354a3–6).

Aristotle distinguishes three kinds of "proofs" or means of persuasion used in the art of rhetoric. The first depends upon character (*ēthos*). An argument gains or loses credibility depending on the character of the one who makes it. Aristotle explains, however, that the persuasive force of character does not derive from any preconceived notion of an individual's worth but is revealed especially through *logos*, that is, through the specific words, ideas, and conceptions used to advance a particular argument (*Rh.* 1.2.1356a4–11). Aristotle departs from other writers on rhetoric by claiming that the revelation of character through speech is almost the "most authoritative" element in persuasion. Secondly, persuasion comes through an audience when the argument stirs their emotions (*pathos*) (*Rh.* 1.2.1356a13–14). Although Aristotle recognizes the importance of placing the audience into a certain frame of mind, he criticizes contemporary writers for devoting almost exclusive attention to this aspect of rhetoric. In doing so, they neglect to treat the third and central ingredient in effective persuasion, namely, the quality of the argument itself. Aristotle identifies a distinctive type of syllogism proper to rhetoric, something that he calls the "*enthymeme*" (*Rh.* 1.1.1355a5–14). Whereas some commentators assume that rhetoric employs defective syllogisms, Arnhart argues persuasively that the *enthymeme* is not syllogistically defective, but rather a particular kind of syllogism.[6] The unique character of the *enthymeme* is found in its reliance upon common opinion, especially those opinions worthy of serious consideration for which Aristotle uses the term *endoxa*. *Endoxa* are "reputable opinions" held by all, by most, or by the wise (*Top.* 100b22–23; see *Rh.* 1.5.1361a25–27). Due to their pervasiveness or the wisdom of those who adhere to them, these opinions enable those who employ them to abbreviate or compress an argument since they establish immediate credibility with a particular audience. Furthermore, such opinions warrant serious attention in their own right because they are likely to contain at least a kernel of truth.[7]

Even Aristotle's most strictly theoretical works begin with an examination of the opinions of his predecessors. It is, however, when he turns to moral-political matters that reputable opinion occupies a central place in the inquiry. In a celebrated passage from the *Nicomachean Ethics*, Aristotle writes:

> As in other cases we must set the phenomena before us and, after first reviewing the puzzles, go on to show, if possible, the truth of all the *endoxa* about these ways of being affected; for if we both resolve the difficulties and leave the *endoxa* standing, we shall have shown our case sufficiently. (7.1.1145b1–7; cf. 1.4.1095a31–95b8; *EE* 1.6.1216b28–35)

A fuller consideration of this passage and its context is offered in chapter 3. The point I wish to emphasize at the outset of this study is that the mode of argument that characterizes Aristotle's treatment of ethics is rhetorical in a fundamental and precise sense. Aristotle takes the reputable opinions of his audience as starting points, examines them in such a way as to make often heterogeneous views more consistent with each other, and brings them to the degree of clarity of which they admit. Insofar as the art of rhetoric begins with reputable opinion, attends to the character and limits of the audience being addressed, and attempts to move its audience in the direction of truth, it seems reasonable to suspect that Aristotle employs this art in his own presentation of politics and ethics. As we shall see, the need for rhetoric arises from Aristotle's attempt to do justice to the competing claims of both virtue and philosophy. In the language of Hesiod and in a way that will be specified in what follows, Aristotle addresses his study both to those able to think things through for themselves and those capable of learning from the arguments of the wise. He will have more to say about the third group (those who neither think for themselves nor take to heart what might be learned from those who do) when he turns to a consideration of actual political practice in the concluding chapter of the study.

## INTERPRETATIVE APPROACH

The book that follows falls between the two genres of literature most usually associated with Aristotelian scholarship. It is neither a line-by-line commentary nor an essay on one or more themes in moral philosophy. As such, I do not attempt to provide the kind of detailed analysis of particular controversies characteristic of more narrowly thematic studies or more expansive and comprehensive ones. Instead, I offer an overview of the *Ethics* which, although it does not enter into every important scholarly dispute, is intended to provide a valuable incentive for doing so by laying bare the rhetorical framework of the text in its present form. *Reading Aristotle's Ethics* elucidates a continuity of argument, or a dimension of that continuity, that has largely eluded scholarly readings because of a more typical preoccupation with specific textual or thematic considerations or because that continuity gets buried in the attempt to supply a general account of the work's manifold discussions. I have fastened on those aspects of Aristotle's inquiry that raise the steepest obstacles to any claim of conceptual unity and have sought to show that attentiveness to the practical purpose and rhetorical design of the book reveals that several apparent discontinuities are better understood as turning points in a comprehensive and comprehensible whole. Although the decision to sketch out an interpretative framework for the entire treatise necessarily precludes in-depth analyses of several important scholarly and textual conundrums, I hope to generate greater appreciation for and interest in the rhetorical dimension of Aristotle's study without claiming to have worked out the consequences of this approach for every important interpretative disagreement. I do so with the expectation that an awareness of this unjustly neglected component of the *Ethics* will prove useful in subsequent attempts to clarify and disentangle its particular themes and notorious problems.

One result of the interpretative approach adopted here is that the argument of the book does not take its bearings from discussions of Aristotle's "development" or various theories about the chronological order of his prolific output. Without denying the validity of these concerns, I believe they are best invoked as a last resort since their premature adoption preempts the discovery of any underlying structural unity that may not be immediately apparent. To take a well-known example, the differences in Aristotle's double treatment of pleasure in Books VII and X are typically attributed to the belief that Book VII is part of the earlier *Eudemian Ethics* whereas the account in Book X belongs to the later *Nicomachean* version. Although this may in fact be the case, the adoption of this explanation discourages further inquiry into possible reasons for the inclusion of both treatments in the text as it now stands. Sloppy or incomplete editing are always possibilities of course, but I suggest an intrinsic and positive reason for the retention of this double treatment, one that derives from the different audiences to which Aristotle addresses his study.

*Reading Aristotle's Ethics* is intended to add to a small but growing body of scholarly literature that maintains the essential cogency of the text as we have it, notwithstanding the very real problems that have given rise to a more pervasive and debilitating fragmentation of the treatise on the part of some of its most serious scholarly students. Despite the magnitude of these discrepancies, the privileged position that this book enjoys within the Western tradition suggests prima-facie evidence of its attractiveness for successive generations of students. This is an observation that I have had the good fortune to corroborate over the course of several years of teaching the *Ethics* to initially perplexed, sometimes resistant, but often appreciative students. From my students I continue to learn about Aristotle's capacity to persuade, provoke, and, on occasion, inspire. I have attempted to navigate the most important scholarly disputes in such a way as to preserve a sense of the difficult and enduring beauty of Aristotle's study. In so doing, I offer a reading of the *Ethics* that puts into sharp relief Aristotle's extraordinary ability to combine sensitivity to the salutary demands of common decency with the sharp and sometimes jarring perspective characteristic of radical inquiry.

# CHAPTER ONE

# The Audience of the *Ethics*, Book I

## THE *ETHICS* IN CONTEXT

It seems reasonable to expect that a comprehensive study of ethics, whatever else it might leave in doubt, would offer a clear teaching on the best way to live as a human being. Yet it is precisely this issue that remains in question in what is arguably the most influential book on ethics ever written. Despite the privileged place that Aristotle's text occupies within the Western tradition, considerable controversy still surrounds the meaning of its central teaching on the best life. The problem is not that Aristotle fails to address this crucial question but that he appears to give two different and perhaps even mutually inconsistent answers.

Whereas the priority that Aristotle assigns to philosophic contemplation over moral virtue is obvious to all students of the *Ethics*, the precise nature of the relationship between them has fired a great deal of debate. Despite the obvious importance of this issue, scholars remain sharply divided. One of the deepest rifts lies between those who maintain that Aristotle argues for some combination of moral and intellectual excellence and those who maintain that his endorsement of contemplative excellence is separable from, and perhaps even incompatible with, his teaching on moral virtue. With varying degrees of difference, the former position is argued by Richard Bodéüs, Stephen Clark, W. F. R. Hardie, Richard Kraut, Carnes Lord, and Amélie Rorty. The latter problem is raised by J. L. Ackrill and Georges Rodier and is given its sharpest expression by John Cooper, Thomas Nagel, and Kathleen Wilkes.

At the very least, continuing controversy about the exact relationship between moral and intellectual virtue in the *Ethics* suggests a certain ambiguity in Aristotle's treatment. I wish to argue that this is a deliberate ambiguity shaped by specific *apologetic* concerns that, at least in part, are responsible for the extraordinary influence of Aristotle's political writings among those who do not primarily or essentially regard themselves as philosophers. Before making this argument, it will prove useful to outline the contours of the debate about Aristotle's teaching on the best life. This dispute both frames the central question of the *Ethics* and points to the need to consider with greater attentiveness the question of Aristotle's intended audience in this book.

## PHILOSOPHIC READINGS OF THE *ETHICS*

At the risk of oversimplifying, it is possible to distinguish two major lines of interpretation concerning Aristotle's teaching on the best life in the *Ethics*. Whereas some detect the presence of two inconsistent views,[1] others argue that Aristotle offers one essentially consistent teaching.[2] Without attempting to exhaust all the nuances in this debate, it is possible to establish the main contours of the problem by summarizing the positions of J. L. Ackrill and John Cooper on the one hand, and of W. F. R. Hardie and Richard Kraut on the other.[3]

Ackrill argues that Aristotle offers an "inclusive" teaching on happiness (*eudaimonia*) in Book I. The primary ingredients of happiness are those activities undertaken for their own sake. When Aristotle concludes that happiness is an activity in accord with the best or most complete virtue, Ackrill observes that nothing in the preceding argument requires or even suggests that we restrict this activity to the contemplative virtue of wisdom (*sophia*). He explains that Aristotle's reference to the best and most complete virtue in Book I points to an inclusive understanding of happiness in that happiness results from the activity of "total virtue," a composite that includes both moral and intellectual excellence.

The difficulty with the inclusive interpretation becomes apparent in the concluding book of the *Ethics* where Aristotle argues that it is not the practice of several moral virtues but the activity of intelligence (*nous*) that constitutes the best and most perfect virtue. Ackrill observes that although Aristotle ranks contemplation above the life of action, his argument in Book X does not assert that what makes an action virtuous is its tendency to promote contemplation. Such an argument would justify even the most "monstrous" activities provided only that they promoted the philosophic life. The problem is that Aristotle offers no alternative explanation as to what makes morally virtuous actions virtuous. He appears to assume that this is self-evident by appealing to the settled character or reliable judgment of decent human beings. This kind of argument, however, offers no principled way of combining Aristotle's emphasis on the intrinsic value of moral virtue throughout the first half of the *Ethics* and the description of contemplation as an "incommensurably more valuable activity" in Book X. The root problem, as Ackrill sees it, is a fundamental lack of clarity in Aristotle's understanding of human nature. Aristotle's failure to present one consistent view of human nature means that his teaching on the best life for human beings is inevitably "broken-backed," that is, "incapable of clear specification even in principle."[4]

John Cooper detects this same tension in Aristotle's teaching on the best life and casts it into sharper relief. Supporting his interpretation with reference to Aristotle's "mature work" in *De Anima*, Cooper maintains that Aristotle adopts an "intellectualist ideal" in Book X, "one in which the highest intellectual powers are split off from the others and made, in some obscure way, to constitute a soul all their own." Aristotle's identification of happiness with contemplation in Book X is so complete that it excludes any concern for familial, social, or political life except insofar as they provide the conditions for a life of theoretical activity. Cooper concludes that Aristotle's considered view of human happiness in Book X does not build upon his analysis of moral virtue in the preceding books but is actually inconsistent with it.[5]

On the other side of this issue Hardie and, more recently, Kraut maintain that the *Ethics* contains a single consistent teaching on the best life.[6] Hardie suggests that Aristotle's arguments in Book I are best compared to preliminary sketches made by an artist before he determinately creates the work of art. If Aristotle is "hesitating" between an "inclusive" and "exclusive" formulation of happiness in Book I, this is not the result of any intellectual confusion on his part but is entirely appropriate given the status of Book I as a "sketch" or "outline" (*perigraphē*). Whereas Ackrill sees an inconsistency in Aristotle's recommendation of wisdom as the dominant ingredient of happiness in Book X and his earlier inclusive recipe for happiness in Book I, Hardie reconciles these differences by emphasizing the tentative character of Book I.

With respect to Aristotle's elevation of the theoretical life in Book X, Hardie maintains that the priority given to the contemplative life is "not so absolute as to make comparison and compromise impossible."

Whereas Aristotle gives "paramount" place in the good life to contemplation, he also retains a place for family, friends, and the active life of the citizen. Aristotle's assertion that the practice of moral virtue yields happiness in a secondary sense is taken by Hardie to confirm this view. He concludes that the *Ethics* teaches the wise to cultivate a variety of goods while giving highest priority to the most fully satisfying activity of theory or science.

Kraut also maintains that the *Ethics* is free of internal conflict, but in doing so he takes issue with both the "intellectualist" and "inclusivist" positions. On the one hand, he argues against the view that happiness consists of contemplative activity *simpliciter* and has, therefore, no intrinsic or necessary connection to the practice of moral virtue. On the other hand, he is critical of interpretations that assert that happiness is a composite of different goods, only one of which is contemplation. Kraut explains that Aristotle offers two good ways of answering the question about happiness. The best answer is that happiness consists in the virtuous activity of theoretical reason (*theōria*). The second best answer is that happiness is to be found in virtuous practical activity, the exercise of virtues such as courage, moderation, and justice. The conflict between these two answers is only apparent. On the one hand, the philosophic life presupposes the development and practice of the ethical virtues, and, on the other, Aristotle "intellectualizes" practical virtues, regarding them as "approximations of the theoretical virtues." In both cases the proper function of human beings is to use reason well. The common core that unites Aristotle's twofold teaching is that human happiness lies *solely* in excellent reasoning activity. This provides the single standard by which the whole range of human actions is to be evaluated. All other goods are or should be desirable only as means to this end; they possess "no direct weight at all in determining how close a person is to happiness or misery."[7]

Although the two main interpretations that emerge from this debate appear irreconcilable, I wish to argue that they point to a deliberate and ultimately consistent tension in Aristotle's ethical teaching. To advance this thesis, it is necessary to bring to light and call into question a common premise shared by many Aristotelian scholars; namely, that the *Ethics* is best understood as a philosophic exposition in the very specific sense that it is intended to present philosophers with a systematic account of the best way of life, one that can and should be analyzed in light of current philosophic discussions on this subject. This points to a second and deeper rift in Aristotelian scholarship, one that arises from the question of Aristotle's intended audience. The issue is not primarily a historical one about the original audience for Aristotle's lectures, but rather a pervasive presumption about the importance and consequences of that audience for understanding and evaluating the nature of Aristotle's study as a whole.

## POLITICAL READINGS OF THE *ETHICS*

A second tradition of scholarly interpretation gives especial weight to the fact that the *Ethics* falls into a group of texts that constitute Aristotle's study of "the human things." These scholars, notwithstanding various interpretative differences, agree in questioning the assumption that every Aristotelian treatise attempts to push out the frontiers of theoretical knowledge. Whatever may be true about Aristotle's studies in physics, biology, or metaphysics, his study of "the human things" is emphatically practical in the sense that it seeks to contribute not only, or even primarily, to theoretical knowledge, but to benefit human life and action. Aristotle's ethical treatises should not be approached as part of a self-contained system, but as part of the more comprehensive and open-ended study of politics to which he assigns them (1.2.1094a26–94b11). As a consequence, an adequate interpretation requires attentiveness to both the rhetorical and pedagogical dimensions of the *Ethics*, a concern that presupposes careful consideration of Aristotle's intended audience.

In the United States, this approach to Aristotle's political writings was pioneered by Leo Strauss and applied to the *Ethics* by Harry Jaffa.[8] Strauss argues that Aristotle founded political science as an independent discipline among other disciplines by clarifying the phenomena of politics from the perspective of the involved citizen, rather than that of the disinterested and scientific observer. From this point of view Aristotle presents moral virtues as they are experienced by those who most embody them; he makes no attempt to deduce virtue from some higher theoretical science, nor does he feel compelled to offer a justification for the widespread belief of decent persons in the intrinsic goodness of moral virtue.[9]

Working within this framework, Jaffa attempts to disentangle the *Ethics* from Aquinas's influential account of that treatise, an account that subsequently came to be all but identified with Aristotle's own view of the subject. Jaffa successfully recovers much of the subtlety and depth of Aristotle's treatment by preserving rather than eliminating several of the ambiguities and apparent inconsistencies that characterize Aristotle's presentation of the moral horizon. Whereas Strauss maintains that Aristotle's treatment of politics is not, strictly speaking, written from a philosophic point of view, Jaffa succeeds in wresting the first part of Aristotle's study of politics from the encroachments of a fundamentally theological perspective. Strauss insists and Jaffa demonstrates the fruitfulness of reading the *Ethics* with an awareness of the citizen perspective within which it was conceived.[10]

More recently, Carnes Lord and Richard Bodéüs have, from different points of view, argued that Aristotle's political works are not intended primarily for philosophers. Lord, writing about the *Politics*, maintains that Aristotle's treatise is neither a strictly political nor strictly philosophic inquiry. The original form of political science articulated by Aristotle occupies a middle ground; it is a practical science that is shaped more by a concern for action than thought. As such it is addressed especially to those who are potential or actual legislators and aims at clarifying and amending their understanding of politics with a view to their greater effectiveness.[11]

Bodéüs applies this view to Aristotle's study of both ethical and political matters, what he considers to be "the entirety of Aristotle's reflections on human things."[12] Bodéüs argues that most of the oral lectures compiled in the *Ethics* were not merely, or even primarily, intended for the full-fledged philosophers of the Lyceum. However, neither were they intended to persuade the as yet unvirtuous to acquire virtue. Although the *Ethics* contains an element of exhortation, it is essentially a collection of analyses aimed at intellectual clarification. Taking his bearings especially from the concluding chapter of the *Ethics*, Bodéüs maintains that the discourses preserved in this book, like those contained in the *Politics*, "are addressed to the person charged with defining the laws, that is, to the politician." Further, each treatise is incomplete without the other. As Aristotle argues in the concluding chapter of the *Ethics*, moral discourse is incapable of establishing virtuous practice among the many who have not already been habituated to virtue. On the other hand, the *Politics* does not provide the kind of moral instruction requisite for legislators who, because they are responsible for education, are, to that degree at least, architects of human happiness. Taking issue with the more pervasive view that the *Ethics* is addressed to those who wish to become virtuous and the *Politics* to those who aspire to political office, Bodéüs maintains that both are intended for those who will preside over the fate of the city. When Aristotle turns to moral and political matters, he is no longer addressing a narrow audience constituted by students of philosophy, but a broader public comprised of those who are especially interested in the problems and issues of political life.

The approach to Aristotle's political writings that takes into account the citizen horizon within which they were conceived has yet to win anything like scholarly consensus. The continued distance between what I have termed philosophic and political readings of the *Ethics* is especially unfortunate given the compelling character of arguments on both sides of the divide. The book that follows is intended to help bridge this chasm by offering a reading of the *Ethics* that works out with greater specificity the implications and consequences of a political reading for our understanding of the treatise in the form in which it has come down to us. I am especially concerned to bring to light what might be called the architectural complexity of the *Ethics*. By this, I mean the structure of the argument as a whole and the pedagogically informed way in which Aristotle conceives and develops particular arguments so as to lead his audience to a greater appreciation for the complexities and tensions inherent in a morally serious life.[13] This, in turn, presupposes attentiveness to the rhetorical design of the book as a whole.


## ARISTOTLE'S DUAL AUDIENCE

Several times at the outset of his consideration Aristotle calls attention to the peculiar character of ethical inquiry (see esp. 1.3.1094b11–95a13 and 2.2.1103b26–04a11). In a striking formulation, Aristotle asserts that the aim of ethical study is not knowledge (*gnōsis*) but action (*praxis*) (1.3.1095a4–6). As he later explains, ethical inquiry, unlike other kinds of study, is not undertaken for the sake of theoretical knowledge (*theōria*) but "so that we might become good" (*hin'agathoi genōmetha*) (2.2.1103b26–30). These opening remarks in Books I and II are echoed in the final chapter of the *Ethics* where Aristotle reminds his readers that in a practical inquiry, the end is not theoretical knowledge but action. Knowing what virtue is, is insufficient because the goal is to possess and practice it, that is, "in some way to become good" (10.9.1179a33–79b4). Aristotle's remarks at the beginning and end of his book effectively frame his study with statements about the peculiar character of this kind of inquiry. Unlike other branches of philosophic investigation, the *Ethics* is explicitly subordinated to a practical rather than theoretical end.

It is especially in light of this practical aim that Aristotle's remarks about the qualities presupposed in his students are fully intelligible. Ethical study is particularly problematic for the young because they lack experience and, hence, the matter about which and from which this study is drawn (1.3.1095a2–6). Moreover, insofar as the young are under the sway of emotion, they make bad students of ethics even if they are capable of understanding the various theoretical principles and definitions that Aristotle sets forth. Since the purpose of the *Ethics* is to help its readers live better lives, those who guide their actions by feelings (*pathos*) derive no real benefit from their merely theoretical knowledge.[14]

Aristotle further indicates that he will assume, as the basis for the discussion that follows, the common (*koinon*) belief that one should act according to right reason (*kata ton orthon logon prattein*) (2.2.1103b31–34). It is important to observe that such a belief is "common" only among those with a decent upbringing. Although Aristotle promises to speak about the exact meaning of this expression later, he makes it clear at the outset that his inquiry is addressed to those who already accept a certain, albeit unspecified, standard of decency (cf. 1.4.1095b2–8; 2.1.1103b23–25).[15] The significance of this condition is best seen by way of contrast. Plato begins his famous dialogue on justice with a powerful assault on the goodness of this virtue. Not only is this attack made by the worldly and cynical Thrasymachus, but it is repeated and expanded by Glaucon and Adeimantus, two brothers who would like to believe that justice is good for the one who practices it but are afraid that such a belief may be naive wishful-thinking. It is precisely this challenge to the goodness of justice in the opening books of the *Republic* that provides the driving force for the imaginative defense that follows. Whereas Plato's dialogue explicitly draws in those readers who are troubled by the most fundamental precondition for a morally decent life—namely, belief in the goodness of moral virtue—there is no comparable beginning in the *Ethics*. Although, as I hope to make clear, Aristotle is acutely aware of this problem and will find a way to broach it later in his study, he begins from a very different starting point. Aristotle assumes that his readers already accept the "orthodox" standard of goodness provided by *orthos logos*. Even without specifying all that is included in such a standard, the comparison to Plato reveals the most essential point. The primary audience of the *Ethics* consists of those who accept rather than question the goodness of virtue itself. It is especially for this audience that Aristotle's study clarifies and to some extent modifies a code of decency that he presupposes on the part of his readers.

Aristotle's preliminary remarks also include a warning to the effect that students of ethics should not expect mathematical precision in a subject dealing with human actions, the just, and the noble (1.3. 1094b19–27). If a certain kind of imprecision is appropriate given the subject of this study, philosophic precision would require that Aristotle challenge the guiding or at least starting premise provided by *orthos logos*. Indeed, the ascent from authoritative opinion to genuine knowledge describes the essential movement of the philosophic life. Nevertheless, Aristotle chooses to begin his study by reflecting and in some sense preserving the kind of noble imprecision characteristic of decent but not necessarily philosophic students.

These initial points might be summarized in the following way. The primary audience of the *Ethics* is characterized less by a desire for theoretical knowledge and more by an attraction to goodness. Hence, those who are beneficiaries of a decent upbringing, have some experience of life, and have attained a certain level of maturity, are in a position to derive the greatest benefit from Aristotle's book and, as such, are its primary, though not necessarily exclusive, addressees. Aristotle's book is not primarily addressed to "philosophers" but to the better sort of persons referred to in classical literature as "gentlemen." Although these two terms—philosopher and gentleman—are generally known, they are used here in a precise way that warrants further clarification.

In its primary and best sense, "gentleman" is a translation of *kalos k'agathos*, a Greek expression meaning "beautiful/noble and good."[16] The term connotes both social-political status and a certain level of moral excellence (*EE* 8.3.1249a10–17). The *kalos k'agathos* is a citizen in the fullest and best sense of the word, one who embodies the highest aims of the polis. He acts with a view to the noble; that is, he both possesses and acts in accordance with those virtues that are generally regarded by decent human beings to be praiseworthy for their own sake (*EE* 8.3.1248b34–38; 1249a1–4). He is also bound to a certain social and political class because his way of life requires both economic well-being and the presence of others in order to practice those virtues that are constitutive of his character.[17] In the *Nicomachean Ethics* Aristotle typically appeals to the "standard" (*kanōn*) or "measure" (*metron*) furnished by the "morally serious" (*ho spoudaios*) or "decent" (*ho epieikēs*) person (consider, among numerous references, 3.4.1113a25–33; 9.9.1170a8–11; 10.5.1176a15–19; and 5.10.1137a34–b2).[18] Although there is a clear overlap between the *spoudaios* and *epieikēs* on the one hand and the *kalos k'agathos* on the other, the latter term carries with it a somewhat narrower connotation in that it is more *directly* tied to a particular social class. As I hope to make clear, Aristotle's appeal to the more inclusive and somewhat ambiguous *spoudaios* and *epieikēs* in the *Nicomachean Ethics* points to the broader dual audience to which this study is directed.

There is, however, a shadow-side to this idealized description of the primary audience of the *Ethics*, one that is reflected in another Greek term used to describe the social-political class with which the *kalos k'agathos* is most closely associated. Aristotle periodically refers to "notables" (*gnōrimoi*). This group is distinguished from the general population by wealth, good birth, virtue, and education (*Pol.* 4.4.1291b28–30). Given the difficulty involved in recognizing genuine virtue, the more visible advantages of wealth, good birth, superior education, and political position provide less ambiguous and more pervasive criteria for distinguishing notables as a social class.[19] Aristotle observes that the more fortuitous advantages of wealth and good birth are very often accompanied by hubris, arrogance or disdain (*Rh.* 2.15–16.1390b14–91a19), and that the *agonistic* love of honor characteristic of the powerful, often expresses itself in domination (*kratein*) (cf. *Rh.* 2.17.1391a20–29 and *Pol.* 7.2.1324b2–7).

As we shall have occasion to see, Aristotle's appeal to the standard provided by the decent or morally serious person should not be simply identified with the more visible and sociological *gnōrimoi*. Although it is true that the notion of the *kalos k'agathos* is drawn from this social group, it is also the case that many, perhaps most, of those properly described as notables fall short of the ideal of *kalokagathia*.[20] The distance between these terms and the different ways in which they are evaluated by Aristotle points to both the rhetorical and pedagogical dimension of his study as a whole. At this point it is sufficient to state what I hope to make clear through subsequent analysis. Aristotle's appeal to the best sensibilities of morally serious persons is not merely a reflection or codification of the current social practice of notables.[21] Although Aristotle's investigation is unquestionably rooted in Greek society, by his own reckoning the value of his study depends upon the adequacy of his analysis of the more enduring aspects of human experience involving character, happiness, and the noble (*Pol.* 7.13.1332a7–25; cf. 3.4.1276b16–77b32).[22]

The nominal definition of the philosopher is one who loves wisdom. In classical usage, philosophy also designates a way of life, one that aims at discovering or "beholding" (*theōria*) the truth. Unlike the *kalos k'agathos*, the philosopher is not bound to any particular social status, nor is his way of life defined in relation to moral excellence. Indeed, as the trial of Socrates revealed, the two ways of life are in serious conflict.[23] Whereas the life of decent persons is circumscribed by social, political, and moral conventions, the philosophic life is characterized by a radical questioning of all conventional beliefs and opinions, even praiseworthy ones, with a view to discovering the truth.

On the basis of these preliminary remarks it is possible to state with greater precision what I take to be a distinctive feature of Aristotle's political writings in general and the *Ethics* in particular. Unlike Aristotle's more explicitly philosophical works (e.g., *Metaphysics* or *Categories*), the *Ethics* takes its bearings from and is addressed to morally serious persons. Moreover, it is simultaneously addressed to two distinct types of morally serious persons: those who are not and never will be philosophers *and* those who are potential philosophers.

It is necessary to add one further qualification to this characterization of the audience of the *Ethics* in light of Aristotle's initial subordination of ethics to politics (1.2.1094a26–b11). Aristotle writes that, whereas it may be valuable to secure the good for a single individual, it is even nobler and more divine to do so for a people and for a city (1.2.1094b9–10). This, Aristotle later explains, is the wish and goal of every decent legislator, namely, to make citizens good by habituating them to virtue through properly framed laws (2.1.1103b3–6). The aim of legislators and the aim of Aristotle's study overlap in this important respect.[24] Viewed in this light, Aristotle's emphasis on a student's need for experience seems to refer especially to political experience (cf. 1.3.1095a2–4). Aristotle's study is directed not only to those who are attracted to moral goodness, but also and perhaps especially to those legislators, or at least potential legislators, with some experience of politics.

Although I agree with Bodéüs on this point, I am not convinced that Aristotle intends to rule out both lower and higher possibilities. There is no reason to assume that Aristotle's writing is one dimensional in the sense that it is *restricted* to lawmakers. Rather, Aristotle also and simultaneously appeals to well-disposed young persons who are drawn to a moral-political excellence they do not yet fully possess (see esp. 2.2.1103b26–30; 10.9.1179b2–4) and, at crucial junctures in his argument, to those who are capable of a type of excellence that in some way transcends the political horizon altogether. The problematic aim of the *Ethics* might be stated in the following way. Aristotle attempts to offer guidance for those who are disposed to an active life of political involvement rather than the rigors and pleasures of philosophic inquiry and who may even view the latter with suspicion. At the same time, however, he will try to point his most gifted students to a way of life that does not fall entirely within the horizon of *orthos logos* by inviting them to contemplate something of the radical and more fully satisfying character of the philosophic life. I hope to show that greater attentiveness to Aristotle's dual audience—nonphilosophers and potential philosophers—reveals an underlying consistency despite the apparent inconsistency attributed to him regarding his teaching on the best way of life.

## THE USEFUL IMPRECISION OF BOOK I

The view that Aristotle is advocating either an "inclusive" or "exclusive" understanding of happiness in the opening book of his study is, I believe, mistaken. A more accurate description of the argument as it stands could affirm that Aristotle moves his readers toward an inclusive view of happiness as a composite of virtuous activities, but that he qualifies this conclusion at the last moment by asserting that happiness consists in the activity of the best or most complete virtue. As Ackrill rightly points out, the reader is unprepared for this twist in Aristotle's argument, but, contrary to Ackrill's interpretation, nothing prevents Aristotle's unexplained qualification in the present context from being an anticipation or foreshadowing of a view that, for pedagogical reasons, he discloses only at a later point in his study. Ackrill fails to give sufficient weight to the fact that the passage in question (esp. 1.7.1098a16–20) is qualified by the immediately following remark. Aristotle maintains that we should allow the argument to serve as an outline and that it provides no more than a rough sketch that can be filled in later (1.7.1098a20–22). Consistent with this qualification, the following overview of Book I reflects a degree of precision (or imprecision) on this issue that Aristotle deems appropriate at the outset of his study.

Happiness or "human flourishing" (*eudaimonia*) is taken by Aristotle to be the good at which all human actions aim (chs. 1–4). His study of ethics seeks to turn students away from diminished understandings of happiness and to direct them toward more humanly satisfying ones. Accordingly, Aristotle takes up the three views of happiness most in evi-

*3 views of happiness*

dence, namely pleasure, honor, and study (ch. 5). In this initial consideration, the life of pleasure seeking is summarily dismissed with a kind of noble disdain, and a consideration of the theoretical life is postponed. By way of contrast, the life of action, particularly political action, is given greater scope. Although Aristotle initially brings readers to the salutary view that virtue rather than honor appears to constitute the appropriate end of political action, he concludes by emphasizing the incompleteness of all three views of happiness and the need for further investigation.

To advance the argument, Aristotle suggests that greater specificity about the nature of human happiness, though not complete clarity, would result from reflection upon a distinctively human activity or "work" (*ergon*) (ch. 7). "Work" along with "end" (*telos*) and "activity" (*energeia*) are used by Aristotle to indicate the characteristic activity of an animate being, one that reveals its specific and irreducible wholeness (cf. *Meta.* 9.8.1050a21–23). Aristotle observes that the distinctive "activity" or "work" of human animals is one that is in accordance with reason (*logos*) or at least not without it (1.7.1098a7–8). Moreover, the best human activity requires not just any expression of reason, but a fine or excellent one. Hence, the good for human beings, the core of human happiness, consists in those activities involving reason that express excellence or possibly several types of excellence (1.7.1098a16–18).[25]

While acknowledging that unforeseen or uncontrollable forces affect the possibility of happiness (e.g., fortune, death, and the gods), the overriding argument of Book I invites readers to focus on the part of happiness that falls within a human compass (chs. 8–12).[26] The aspect of happiness that depends preeminently on human effort is the development and exercise of each individual's capacity for excellence. This, Aristotle teaches, constitutes a core without which happiness is not attainable for a human being. The books that follow differentiate and clarify the particular excellences, both moral and intellectual, that perfect the human soul and, to that extent, constitute human happiness.

The foregoing sketch of Book I preserves the adumbrative quality of the argument as it is presented by Aristotle. The argument is imprecise, however, in a way that is especially appropriate given the didactic concern that guides the study as a whole. By suggesting the problematic character of the most common views concerning happiness, Aristotle invites his readers to think seriously about a question that many take for granted. Further, instead of launching a doctrine of his own, Aristotle has suggested two orientation points that are conducive to serious reflection: happiness for human beings involves both reason (*logos*) and excellence (*aretē*). To state this negatively, the failure to develop one's capacities for both reason and excellence precludes the possibility of lasting happiness notwithstanding the many advantages that turn upon wealth, good birth, status, and power.

Aristotle's argument in Book I is compelling as far as it goes. It is hard to see how activities that fail to engage reason or are poorly carried out could result in lasting human happiness. Whatever philosophic difficulties are caused by Aristotle's imprecision, particularly, his failure to clarify the metaphysical or psychological premises of the *ergon* argument or to specify whether *eudaimonia* is a composite of virtues or a single dominant virtue, the argument is not only intelligible to decent and thoughtful readers, but invites them to wonder about the relationship between reason and excellence and the exact bearing of each on happiness. Moreover, since happiness results from the development or perfection of the human soul, and each of the virtues—moral and intellectual—contributes to that perfection, the open-ended character of Aristotle's treatment of happiness in Book I leads the reader to assume, initially at least, that *all* the virtues described in the following books of the *Ethics* are essential ingredients of human happiness.[27] Prior to his concluding argument in Book X, Aristotle exercises judicious silence about the exact relationship between moral and intellectual virtue. This restraint is not without an important pedagogical consequence since it allows Aristotle to elucidate the nature of moral virtue from the perspective of those who most embody it, those who, I have suggested, constitute the primary audience of the *Ethics*.

By taking his bearings from the best sensibilities of decent readers, Aristotle encourages greater reflectiveness, not by undermining decent opinion, but by presenting it with unprecedented clarity. As we shall see, this approach characterizes Aristotle's treatment of the particular moral virtues and gives rise to some of the most memorable and best known aspects of that teaching. Aristotle's doctrine of the "mean" is a case in point. An even more pertinent example is his repeated insistence that moral virtue is an end in itself and desirable for its own sake. Not only is this approach likely to appeal to and elevate the perspective of Aristotle's readers, it also provides a true depiction of the phenomenon of moral virtue itself. To present moral virtue as a means to some other end, or as derivative from metaphysical or psychological principles, would distort that phenomenon as it appears in the lives of those who most embody it.

The way in which Arisotle presents moral virtue does not necessarily imply that his ethical teaching is devoid of any theoretical grounding.[28] Rather, the point is that Aristotle's solicitude for the majority of his decent readers requires that this derivation, should it exist, occupy a less than prominent place given the practical aim that he has assigned to his study. The result is a consideration of virtue and happiness that is both accessible to decent readers and, for the same reason, susceptible to accusations of inconsistency on the part of the most philosophic among them. Whatever apparent inconsistency is provoked by this approach, it is important to recognize that Aristotle's manner of proceeding is in fact perfectly consistent with the goal that he has set for his study: the *Ethics* aims less at imparting theoretical knowledge about human goodness and more at reinforcing and clarifying it, especially for those most keenly interested in invigorating the practice of virtue among fellow citizens.

# CHAPTER TWO

# The Virtues,
# Books II–VI

## THE DOCTRINE OF ETHICAL VIRTUE

By far, the bulk of Aristotle's discussion of virtue is given over to a consideration of what he calls ethical virtue (*ēthikē aretē*) (Bks. II-V). Ethical or, as they are typically called, moral virtues pertain especially to character. Using an analogy to the arts that he later qualifies, Aristotle explains that excellence of character, like excellence in musical performance, is developed through practice. Just as one becomes an accomplished pianist by playing the piano, so one becomes just by doing just acts. When such practices become habitual, they constitute the fixed disposition or character (*hexis*) that, more than anything else, determines an individual's identity. The development of excellence in character is the high aim of the legislator's art since, Aristotle asserts, the aim of all good legislation is to make citizens good by training them in good habits (2.1.1103b3–6). Parents, legislators, and Aristotle's study of ethics share the common aim of encouraging habits conducive to goodness (2.1.1103b23–25; 2.2.1103b26–31).

Whereas Aristotle had originally dismissed the life devoted to pleasure in Book I (1.5.1095b19–22), he now indicates that ethical virtue is especially concerned with pleasure and pain (2.3.1104b8–9). Pleasure and pain are the standards by which all, to a greater or lesser degree, regulate their actions and, as such, a serious consideration of them is essential to the study of both virtue and politics (2.3.1105a3–13). This is the second kind of consideration of pleasure that Aristotle provides in the *Ethics*, one that gives it considerably more scope than his first.[1] Pleasure and pain are taken up as topics for serious consideration insofar as they bear on the development of character. To anticipate part of Aristotle's teaching, this second type of consideration stands as a "mean" between an initial disdainful dismissal of the life devoted to pleasure in Book I and a more rigorous treatment of pleasure as an end in itself in Book VII. The concern for pleasure reenters Aristotle's consideration, but as part of a primary concern to elucidate and foster the development of ethical virtue.[2]

Aristotle begins to confront the paradox implicit in his analysis so far. If one becomes virtuous by doing virtuous deeds, then the process of becoming virtuous seems to presuppose the possession of virtue (2.4.1105a17–21).[3] Aristotle explains by qualifying his earlier comparison between virtue and art. Whereas the success of an art or skill resides exclusively in the outcome (a well-performed piece of music or properly built home), ethical virtue is not gauged simply by the final action but is also determined by the state of mind from which the action springs. A virtuous act is done knowingly, chosen deliberately for its own sake, and arises from a fixed disposition (2.4.1105a31–33). Hence, while it is neither necessary nor possible to *possess* virtue in order to become virtuous, one can and must cultivate the external actions appropriate to virtue as a part of the process of becoming genuinely virtuous. Aristotle's earlier emphasis on the centrality of correct opinion and proper education becomes, with this explanation, more fully intelligible. These exert a powerful influence on the type of actions that become habitual and, as such, provide the indispensable ground for the development of full virtue. Aristotle criticizes the widespread human tendency to argue about rather than act upon virtue, a tendency rooted in the belief that ethical knowledge is sufficient to insure moral seriousness (2.4.1105b12–18). It is not enough to recognize the principles that emerge from philosophic debate. However true they may be, they are helpful only in the measure that they are also expressed in deed. The acquisition of ethical virtue cannot be identified with either art or philosophy; practice apart from rational deliberation or rational deliberation apart from practice fails to achieve the desired state. At the same time, however, ethical virtue is presented as partaking, to some extent at least, in both art and philosophy since both habitual conduct and rational deliberation are necessary for its development.

Ethical virtue then is a deliberately cultivated disposition that is characterized by attaining a certain kind of mean (*mesotēs tis*), that which lies between excess and deficiency as these pertain to emotion and action. The mean is discovered through the use of reason such as it is exercised by a prudent person (*phronimos*) (2.6.1106b36–07a2). Aristotle's definition borrows the concept of the mean from mathematics. As applied to ethics, however, the mean is not characterized by strict arithematical proportion but is "relative to us" (*pros hēmas*), in the sense that it is determined with reference to the particular capacities and limitations of the person undertaking any given action. Whereas we should expect that specific actions constituting the mean will vary from one individual and situation to another, Aristotle maintains that ethical virtue consistently possesses the character of a mean, at least with respect to its substance (*ousia*). With respect to the highest good (*to ariston*) and doing well (*to eu*), ethical virtue is an extreme (*akrotēs*) (2.6.1107a6–8). Finally, Aristotle notes that not every action or emotion admits of a mean. There is, for example, no such thing as committing adultery with the right person, at the right time, and in the right manner, since the very act of adultery is itself base.

Aristotle concludes his general consideration of ethical virtue with an account of "the voluntary" that culminates in several surprisingly straightforward affirmations. Most broadly, ethical virtues and their corresponding vices are part of the voluntary and, as such, belong to the range of things that fall within our power (3.5.1113b3–21). More specifically, it is ultimately a matter of our own doing whether we become decent or base, a view implicit in the notion of reward and punishment (3.5.1113b21–30). Using a medical analogy, Aristotle likens "vices of the soul" to diseases of the body (3.5.1114a11–31). Although our capacity for health is severely restricted once a disease has reached an advanced state, we are still responsible for those practices that caused us to contract the disease in the first place. Aristotle concludes that we are also responsible for what we perceive as the good to be pursued in action, since this too is a function of the character we have developed (3.5.1114a31–b25).

Aristotle's endorsement of human responsibility is, however, more nuanced than may first appear.[4] Reflection on the central medical analogy begins to suggest why. Although some diseases may result from actions of our own choosing, others are congenital or result from improper care in childhood. Given the importance of early education for the development of ethical virtue, Aristotle's explicit argument ought not to be construed in a rigid or absolute manner. Nevertheless, Aristotle affirms a politically useful standard from which individuals and lawmakers can take their bearings. In those cases where one is not born with a defective nature and has received some kind of decent upbringing, the shaping of one's character is, in some significant way, in one's own hands.[5]

Aristotle's general discussion of ethical virtue is followed by a thematic consideration of each particular virtue. Emotions, external goods, and social relationships furnish the raw matter for ethical virtue since it is possible to deal with these universal ingredients of human experience in a better or worse manner. However, Aristotle's initial catalogue and subsequent discussion of each virtue is not quite what the reader has been led to expect. The particular considerations turn out to contain several irregularities that do not entirely fit within the general framework he has provided. Most notable among these, neither of the two peaks of ethical virtue—magnanimity and justice—can be understood as mean states in an unqualified sense. Shame (*aidōs*) is both denied the status of a virtue and described as a mean. Righteous indignation (*nemesis*) is included in the catalogue but mysteriously drops out of Aristotle's consideration in the following chapters.[6] While Aristotle's account introduces unprecedented clarity into the sphere of ethical virtue, it is not mathematical clarity. Indeed, both the initial framework and the particular considerations that follow, should be read in light of Aristotle's twice repeated injunction not to impose greater precision than is appropriate to the matter under investigation (1.3.1094b11–27; 2.2.1103b34–04a11). A proper treatment of ethical virtue should, in Aristotle's view, preserve rather than eliminate the tensions inherent in ethical phenomena itself.

## ASCENT TO MAGNANIMITY

Aristotle begins his discussion of the particular ethical virtues in a way that follows the schema he has set down. Courage and moderation both deal with emotions or feelings. He then considers actions involving the proper use of external goods in his discussions of generosity and generosity on a large scale, a virtue he calls magnificence. However, when he turns to a consideration of "greatness of soul" or "magnanimity" (*megalopsuchia*), he departs from his original design. Aristotle does not present this virtue from a single point of view. He chooses instead to provide his readers with a multifaceted portrait of the magnanimous person. If it is possible to liken Aristotle's treatment of ethical virtue to schematic paintings, the discussion of magnanimity is best compared to sculpture. In the same way that one views a statue by walking around it, Aristotle invites readers to ponder the magnanimous person from several different and even conflicting points of view.

The account of magnanimity is riddled with ambiguity and, not surprisingly, has given rise to widely diverse interpretations. Scholarly assessments of what Aristotle is doing in this discussion range from the solemn to the comic, from a portrait of the rare excellence embodied in the philosopher (Gauthier and perhaps Aspasius) to an ironical rendering of the views of ordinary Greeks (Burnet, Dirlmeier).[7] I hope to show that some of the interpretative difficulty surrounding this controversial peak derives from a well-intentioned but misguided attempt to flatten Aristotle's discussion in such a way as to render it more immediately consistent with itself and Aristotle's more typical manner of proceeding in this part of his treatise.

Whereas the initial catalogue of ethical virtues describes magnanimity as a mean concerning honor and dishonor (2.7.1107b21–23), the thematic discussion does not. Greatness, not honor, is the measure of the magnanimous person.[8] Magnanimous persons believe themselves to be worthy of great things and really are (4.3.1123b1–2). Not only do they possess all of the virtues, but they possess what is great in each one of them (4.3.1123b30). Only with difficulty is greatness made to fit within the schema of the mean, and it is not the kind of mean that we have been led to expect, one dealing with feelings, actions, or external goods. Magnanimity is a mean between vanity and small-mindedness; that is, it characterizes those who have a proper appreciation of their true worth, provided that their worth is great. Whereas magnanimity must be considered an extreme with respect to greatness, it is a mean between excessive and defective self-love or, in modern parlance, self-esteem.

Aristotle passes up the opportunity to fit magnanimity more neatly into his general design by distinguishing it from a separate and nameless virtue that is defined as a mean with respect to honors, absenting the element of greatness (4.4.1125b1–25). Although magnanimous persons also exhibit the proper attitude toward honors, this proves to be the result of their primary attachment to nobility and goodness (*kalokagathia*) (4.3.1124a3–4). Magnanimous persons accept great honors conferred upon them by exceptional persons as their due, and even less than their due, since there is no honor worthy of complete virtue (*pantelēs aretē*) (4.3.1124a6–9). Just as honors bestowed on gods are thought to be pleasing to them, not because they are commensurate with divine excellence but because they are the best that human beings can offer, great honors bestowed on magnanimous persons elicit moderate pleasure. Two statements to the effect that the magnanimous are primarily interested in honor (4.3.1123b19–24 and 1124a5–12) need to be understood in context. With respect to "external goods," magnanimous persons aim most at honor because it is the greatest good of this kind. This concern with the external good of honor is, however, subordinate to a more interior preoccupation with virtue itself, something that is indicated by the fact that such an individual derives only moderate pleasure from even great honors, and in that case only if they are conferred by morally serious persons (4.3.1124a5–7). Although magnanimous persons are not characterized by Socratic indifference to honor, neither do they regard it as the greatest good (4.3.1125a16–17); in fact, Aristotle maintains that honor seems to them to be something small (*mikron*) (4.3.1125a29). Magnanimous persons are sensitive to the place and importance of honors without, however, making them the central concern of their lives.

The attitude of magnanimous persons toward external goods is presented in a similar way. They are neither excessively pleased nor excessively pained by good and ill fortune (4.3.1124a13–16). Good birth, wealth, and power are typically valued for the honors they procure, but since honor is a small thing for magnanimous persons, the goods that elicit honor are even further removed from their core concern. This lofty detachment from both the goods of fortune and honor causes magnanimous persons to appear haughty (*huperoptēs*) (4.3. 1124a19–20). Aristotle responds in two ways. First, he does not deny that the results of good fortune contribute to magnanimity (4.3. 1124a20–21), but only that such goods provide a basis for human greatness. Secondly, many are thought to be magnanimous who are not. Unable to imitate the extraordinary virtue of the great, they imitate only their lofty detachment, affecting a greatness they do not possess since their pretense rests on nothing other than the greater amount of external goods within their possession. Aristotle's distinction can be expressed in the following way. The superiority of the magnanimous person is the result of *looking up* to nobility and goodness (*kalokagathia*), compared to which a preoccupation with honors and the goods of fortune appears inferior and unworthy. The lofty detachment of the magnanimous person derives from a more fundamental attachment.[9] By way of contrast, pretenders to magnanimity attempt to convince themselves of a superiority they cannot legitimately claim by *looking down* upon others on the basis of their greater good luck. The substitution of greatness in external goods for greatness in virtue does not produce magnanimity, but rather arrogance and hubris.

This rendition of the magnanimous person has much in common with the idealized beauty of classical sculpture. The last section of Aristotle's discussion, however, suggests that even this peak of nobility is fashioned with feet of clay. Aristotle concludes by describing several characteristics of ambiguous attractiveness (4.3.1124b5–25a17). Magnanimous persons enjoy benefiting others but tend to forget favors received. Whereas they are willing to take risks for a great cause, they are more typically idle and slow to act. They have trouble adjusting their lives to others, with the possible exception of friends. They are not prone to wonder since they find nothing great and are not given to praising others. They prefer to possess beautiful and unprofitable things rather than useful ones since these accord better with self-sufficiency. Finally, they are characterized by slow movements, a deep voice, and firm speech. Aristotle's final solemn touches seem comically applied. Even if it is possible to defend each of these outward attributes by connecting them to the more substantial interior state from which they derive,[10] it is hard to escape the impression that Aristotle's concluding remarks are meant to engender ironic distance on the part of the reader.

Aristotle simultaneously invites and withdraws admiration for this peak of ethical virtue. Insofar as magnanimous persons look up to nobility and goodness, they properly stand as models for those who fall below them. But insofar as Aristotle emphasizes the more external attributes associated with those most often thought to embody political greatness, he invites his readers to look upon these characteristics with something less than reverence.

## THE IDENTITY OF THE MAGNANIMOUS PERSON

The ambivalence of Aristotle's portrait is heightened by raising an apparently innocent question regarding the identity of the magnanimous person. Does Aristotle's description refer to political greatness or philosophic excellence? The question proves more difficult to answer than one might initially expect, a difficulty compounded by Aristotle's reference to magnanimity in the *Posterior Analytics*.

In the relevant passage (*Pos. An.* 2.13.97b16–24), Aristotle is concerned to elucidate the problem posed by using words that possess two or more different meanings. The problem is illustrated with the example of magnanimity. On the one hand, taking one's bearings from Alcibiades, Achilles, and Ajax, the magnanimous person is characterized by unwillingness to endure dishonor. On the other hand, insofar as this virtue is exhibited by Lysander and Socrates, it refers to equanimity in good and bad fortune. Aristotle goes on to explain that if there is nothing that is the same in these two definitions, there will be two "species" or "kinds" (*eidē*) of magnanimity.

The first type of magnanimity represented by Alcibiades, Achilles, and Ajax is explicitly political. All three exemplars embody a conception of greatness that expresses itself in action and battle. Each is characterized by a desire for glory that exhibits itself in conquest and implacable resistance to dishonor. The second kind of magnanimity is more ambiguous since it embraces both a Spartan general and an Athenian philosopher. Lysander certainly endured the reversals of fortune (from the height of military renown after his victory over Athens in the Peloponnesian War to eventual humiliation, abandonment, and defeat at the hands of the Spartan kings), but there is a considerable question about the extent of his equanimity. It may be that Lysander is included as a more accessible but less perfect introduction to the less accessible but more perfect attribute of magnanimity exemplified by Socrates. Although Plato does not refer to magnanimity, he does have Socrates speak of philosophic magnificence. As part of his account of philosophic virtue, Socrates explains that nothing human seems great, and even death itself is not terrible for one who contemplates all being and all time (*Rep.* 486a–b). Insofar as Socrates bears the vicissitudes of fortune more perfectly than Lysander, Aristotle appears to suggest that the second kind of magnanimity is, at root, philosophic.[11]

It should not go unnoticed that all of the exemplars chosen by Aristotle to illustrate either type of magnanimity find themselves to be in conflict with their fellow citizens. Both Alcibiades and Lysander subordinate political allegiance to personal ambition in turning against democratic Athens and the Spartan monarchy respectively. The dishonor that caused Achilles to withdraw from battle resulted in the death of many fellow Greeks, and similarly, the dishonor at the root of Ajax's madness and suicide deprived the Greeks of a great warrior. Although Socrates' situation belongs to a different order, his remoteness from the sensibilities of democratic Athens resulted in condemnation and death. Despite the existence of different types of magnanimity, the aspiration to human greatness finds itself, on some level at least, in tension with citizen virtue and concern for the common good. Considered from the point of view of what is necessary to sustain healthy political life, the claim that any of these figures embodies the peak of human excellence is not beyond question.

I would suggest that it is precisely these two sources of ambiguity—namely, the uncertain identity of the magnanimous person and the tension between human greatness and healthy political life—that best explains the perplexing character of Aristotle's account of this virtue in the *Ethics*.

With respect to the identity of the magnanimous person, Gauthier's erudite study claims to see a development in Aristotle's thinking on this issue from his earlier treatment in the *Posterior Analytics* to his more mature reflection in the *Nicomachean Ethics*. Gauthier maintains that Aristotle's earlier equivocation has given way to a single conception of magnanimity, one that is consistently fashioned with Socrates as its most perfect exemplar.[12] On the other side of the issue, Hardie argues convincingly that Aristotle's account in the *Ethics* describes a magnanimity that reveals itself in political and military actions, both of which are later said to be "distinguished by nobility and greatness" (10.7. 1177b16–17).[13] I think there is merit, although unequal, in both of these views and that Aristotle's account is deliberately open ended.

Several aspects of Aristotle's discussion point to the kind of extraordinary virtue required for political greatness. In addition to the location of this discussion within his consideration of the ethical virtues, Aristotle includes several specific traits that pertain directly to political life. The magnanimous person undertakes great and notable deeds, is willing to face great dangers, confers great benefits, and is eager to provide help to others. I believe Hardie is correct in maintaining that the preponderance of weight in Aristotle's portrait tips in favor of political greatness. Still, the account does include features that seem more characteristic of philosophers than statesmen. In addition to the persistent and troublesome remoteness that pervades Aristotle's portrait as a whole, the magnanimous person is characterized by deliberate idleness, a preference for truth over opinion, an inclination to irony, and an almost godlike aspiration to self-sufficiency. Aristotle is silent about both dedicated action on behalf of the common good and the philosophic activity of contemplation. The inclusion of either of these attributes would have done much to dispel the enigma of a portrait that does not fit entirely into one camp but is, in some sense, a composite of both. Aristotle refers to the political and philosophic ways of life as the two ways of life chosen by those most ambitious for virtue (*hoi philotimotatoi pros aretēn*) (*Pol.* 7.2.1324a29–32). Arnhart expresses the situation well when he observes that "Aristotelian magnanimity has two faces, one political and one philosophic."[14]

The open-ended character of Aristotle's portrait of human greatness in the *Ethics* is consistent with the open-ended character of his teaching on human happiness in Book I. Greatness, like happiness, is an activity involving virtue and if there are several, it accords with the best and most perfect. Aristotle's portrait, though it leans toward the more visible and popular political conception of human greatness, does not foreclose other possibilities. The pedagogical effect of this first level of ambiguity regarding the identity of the magnanimous person is that it enables Aristotle to direct his readers to a conception of human greatness that, to some degree at least, incorporates features from two ways of life that will be sharply distinguished and ranked only at a later point in his study.

Despite the more philosophic elements that Aristotle has added to his discussion and notwithstanding the valiant efforts of Gauthier to the contrary, Aristotle's account points with least uncertainty to the life of political heroes. It is, I believe, this fact that accounts for the second layer of ambiguity in his presentation, namely, the initially sublime but finally ironic light that he shines on his subject. In this respect, it is helpful to think of the particular exemplars of this virtue in the *Posterior Analytics*. The ambivalence of Aristotle's portrait reflects his deeper ambivalence for the code of the gentleman as it is revealed in the lives of Alcibiades, Achilles, Ajax, and even Lysander.[15] His barely concealed irony for the reverence typically accorded to the politically powerful both by others and themselves seems calculated to alter the preoccupation of "notables" (*gnōrimoi*) with honor, victory, and conquest. By casting the limitations of the more popular version of this ideal in an unattractive light, Aristotle gently ridicules the foibles of a kind of ambition that ultimately proves destructive to both human greatness and healthy political life, as the political exemplars in the *Posterior Analytics* make all too clear. It is when magnanimity is severed from its substantial core that Aristotle ironically depicts the empty outer shell of only apparently magnanimous behavior. By making nobility the central concern of the magnanimous person, Aristotle appeals to the best sensibilities of morally serious and politically ambitious readers. The dignity that he attributes to the political hero stems not from good birth, wealth, or power, however necessary these may be for the execution of great deeds. Neither does it stem from a primary preoccupation with the honors that come from victory and conquest. True greatness of soul may prove to be less dependent on the goods of fortune than is commonly thought. Indeed, it may have less to do with victorious conquest and political power than Aristotle's primary audience is as yet disposed to believe.[16]

## JUSTICE: COMPREHENSIVE VIRTUE AND PROPORTIONAL EQUALITY

The reader gradually descends from the lofty summit of magnanimity through a consideration of two virtues, one concerned with small honors and the second with anger. The discussion passes through the valley of daily social interactions (friendliness, truthfulness, wit, and the non-virtue of shame) before ascending to the second and final peak in the treatment of ethical virtue. Aristotle's consideration of ethical virtue culminates in a discussion of justice to which he devotes an entire book.

This treatment begins by noting a subtle equivocation in speech about justice which obscures the fact that it possesses two distinct meanings. The first meaning of justice refers to "complete" or "perfect" virtue. This understanding is evidenced when we refer to someone as a just person, meaning that the individual in question possesses the several attributes associated with goodness. Justice in this sense is comprehensive virtue in that it includes all the ethical virtues (5.1.1129b25–30). The second meaning of justice refers to one species of virtue within the genus provided by justice understood as comprehensive virtue. In this sense, justice is one particular ethical virtue among others, on a par with courage, temperance, or liberality. I will depart slightly from scholarly convention by referring to justice in the first sense as "comprehensive justice," while retaining the standard "particular justice" to denote its second meaning.[17]

Aristotle distinguishes comprehensive from particular justice by turning to the most visible cases of injustice. Injustice is most in evidence when someone breaks the law or when "grasping" individuals take more than their fair share. Conversely, the two primary senses of justice are "the lawful" (*to nomimon*) and the "equal" or "fair" (*to ison*) (5.1.1129a32–b1).

Comprehensive justice, that is, complete or perfect virtue, is initially identified with law-abidingness (5.1.1129b19–25; 5.2.1130b18–24).[18] Although this seemingly exaggerated claim on behalf of law is foreign to modern sensibilities, it is necessary to recall that Aristotle's conception of the purpose of law differs significantly from that which prevails today. Whereas citizens of liberal democracies tend to look upon law as a neutral authority that secures the life, safety, and individual liberties of those that fall under its protective shield, Aristotle insisted on the formative power of law for shaping the souls of citizens. If the civic association comes into being for the sake of living, it exists for the sake of living well (*Pol.* 1.2.1252b29–30). Since some shared notion of the good life is the end of the polis, the laws do more than hold it together; they also aim at making citizens good and just (*Pol.* 3.9.1280b67–12; cf. 3.9.1280b39–81a4). In the present context, Aristotle explains that law prescribes a certain conduct. For example, the law commands courageous, temperate, and gentle actions while, at the same time, prohibiting the corresponding vices of cowardice, adultery, and violent retaliation. Hence, rightly enacted law commands all the virtues and forbids all the vices (5.1.1129b19–25; 5.2.1130b22–25). It is in this sense that justice as comprehensive virtue is identified with law-abidingness.

Aristotle qualifies this conclusion in a way that is crucial for understanding the perspective that informs his treatment of justice as a whole. Justice is perfect virtue, not simply, but insofar as it is directed toward others (*all' ouch haplōs alla pros heteron*) (5.1.1129b25–30a14).[19] It is the other-oriented nature of justice that causes it to be regarded as the "chief" (*kratistē*) virtue, "more wondrous than morning or evening star." Not only does rightly enacted law command all the virtues but it does so with a view to the common good. Law provides an education toward the common life that fosters the development of comprehensive virtue toward others (5.2.1130b25–26). Justice in this sense is not a part but the whole of virtue (*holē aretē*) (5.2.1130a8–9), and in some way rivals the status earlier conferred upon magnanimity.[20] Both of the peaks in Aristotle's treatment of ethical virtue deal with comprehensive virtue, but they do so from two different points of view—from the point of view of individual greatness and from the point of view of one's relationship with others, particularly one's fellow citizens. Aristotle's initial account of justice as comprehensive virtue reveals the second axis around which his consideration of human excellence turns; namely, one's relations with others as part of a political community. The essentially political character of human being profoundly, although not exclusively, determines both the nature and possibility of human excellence and even human happiness (5.1.1129b17–19; cf. 1.2.1094a26–94b11; *Pol.* 1.1–2.1252a1–53a39).

If the initial exalted discussion of justice as comprehensive virtue recalls his earlier treatment of magnanimity, the bulk of Aristotle's text is given over to a consideration of particular justice, that is, the second and narrower understanding of justice as the equal or fair (*to ison*). Particular justice also concerns one's relation to others and is divided into two kinds. The first, distributive justice (*to dianemētikon dikaion*), apportions the divisible assets of the political community, especially money and honor, on the basis of some predetermined standard of merit (free birth, wealth, good birth, virtue). It is defined by Aristotle as proportional equality (*analogia isotēs*) involving at least four terms, where the goods distributed are proportionate to the merit of the ones receiving them. The second kind of particular justice is called corrective justice (*to diorthōtikon dikaion*) and bears especially on private transactions. Justice in this sense regards all parties as equal and seeks to rectify injustice by restoring an equality that is calculated in terms of loss and gain. With the application of corrective justice, the one suffering loss recovers an amount equal to that possessed before the transgression.

Both forms of particular justice presuppose some measure of reciprocity (*to antipeponthos*). Reciprocity is the glue that holds the political community together (5.5.1131b32–33a2). The exchange of unlike goods is the obvious and necessary condition for the existence of the polis, and the inability to exchange punishment for evils endured causes individuals to think of themselves as slaves rather than citizens (5.5.1132b34–33a1). Reciprocal justice proves to be the indispensable ground of the political association. It is based on proportional equality and uses money as a conventional measure to establish commensurability between unlike goods, services, and transgressions.

Justice, in either its comprehensive or particular meaning, does not easily fit into the schema of the mean. Whereas each of the other ethical virtues is a mean between two vices, this is not true for justice, which is described as a mean between doing and suffering injustice (5.5.1133b30–32). While doing injustice typically stems from the "graspingness" (*pleonexia*) of someone overly concerned with gain, the same cannot be said about suffering injustice since this does not necessarily imply vice on the part of the one who suffers it (see 5.11.1138a31–35). Aristotle's description of the mean is, however, appropriate given the distinctive character of justice as a whole. Justice is virtue "toward others" and is especially concerned with the public good of the political community. Aristotle's analysis of justice appropriately assumes the point of view of the city or, at least, the legislator since this is the sphere proper to justice itself. Viewed from this perspective justice is precisely the kind of mean that Aristotle has described. Justice is present in the city in the measure that relations among citizens are regulated by proportional equality such that both doing and suffering injustice are absent.

The abstract, even mathematical nature of Aristotle's analysis of distributive, corrective, and reciprocal justice clarifies the principles of particular justice in a way that suggests their universality. At the same time, however, it obscures or at least softens a major shift in Aristotle's treatment. The initial exaltation of justice as comprehensive virtue toward others has given way to a sober preoccupation with the less than noble necessities that constrain public life. Disputes about justice typically center around the public allocation of divisible resources such as wealth and honor, or private conflicts involving property, personal injury, and violence (5.2.1130b30–31a9). Rarely do legal disputes provoke deliberations about competing notions of human excellence. Instead of a protracted discussion of the sordid content of litigation to which he only alludes, Aristotle provides a mathematical analysis of the underlying proportions by which legal contests can be justly mediated, a strategy that does not call attention to the necessarily lower horizon within which the account of particular justice is given. The concern for others that is the hallmark of justice requires a level of virtue not beyond the reach of ordinary citizens. In sharp contrast to his earlier portrait of the magnanimous person, Aristotle's elucidation of particular justice reveals the lowest common denominator for justice in the city. The initial elevation of justice is gradually superseded by a consideration of the nonheroic principles that furnish the rudimentary bonds of the political association.

## THE PROBLEM OF POLITICAL JUSTICE

The extent to which Aristotle has reflected an initial exaggerated view of comprehensive justice becomes apparent in each of his subsequent considerations of political justice (chs. 6–7), the voluntary (chs. 8–9), and equity and psychic justice (chs. 10–11). To draw on a famous Platonic metaphor, Aristotle's discussion in these chapters can, like Socrates' political reforms in *Republic V*, be likened to three waves that effectively wear down the privileged status enjoyed by justice at the outset of the consideration.

The first wave to break upon the comprehensive virtue of law-abidingness emerges from the distinction between "political justice" (*to politikon dikaion*) and "the simply just" (*to haplōs dikaion*) (5.6.1134a24–26). Political justice exists between free and equal persons living a common life for the purpose of satisfying their needs (5.6.1134a26–30). The mutual relations of citizens are regulated by law, which guarantees the kind of simple or proportional equality requisite for life in the polis (5.6.1134a30–b2; 1134b8–15). Aristotle, however, also affirms the existence of natural justice and, corresponding to it, one best form of government (5.7.1135a3–5). If it is true that natural justice is unchanging among the gods, among human beings, Aristotle asserts, all justice is variable (5.7.1134b28–30). Consequently, natural justice cannot be identified with human laws and, even in the best case, the variability of justice among human beings bespeaks deficiency. Even the best laws of the best regime fall short of commanding all virtue and forbidding all vice. Aristotle's argument does not deny that law can provide an education to virtue, but suggests the necessarily limited capacity of law to achieve so lofty an aim.

The problem stems from the fact that law does not look toward virtue from the point of view of virtue itself (i.e., the noble or what befits the noble), but rather from the point of view of political justice. It is the various species of particular justice (distributive, corrective, and reciprocal) that actually prevail in the city and each of these is animated by a concern for "the equal" (*to ison*) rather than for "excellence" (*aretē*).[21] Justice, as it actually exists in cities, is described as a kind of proportion that aims at establishing or restoring some kind of equality. Insofar as law educates citizens to comprehensive virtue, that education takes its bearings from the needs of the city. Whether such an education fosters an adequate appreciation for the highest human excellence is open to question. In most decent regimes the potential conflict between the good of the regime, as it is understood by those who rule, and the good of the individual is minimized but not eliminated. The problem is made explicit in the *Politics* where Aristotle considers the case posed by an individual (or group of individuals) so outstanding in virtue as to destroy the kind of equality necessary for life in the polis (*Pol.* 3.13.1284a3–15; cf. 3.17.1288a15–29). Such individuals cannot properly be considered a part of the city since they are done an injustice if deemed worthy of a status that is in some way equal to those who fall far below them in merit. Aristotle describes a godlike human excellence that destroys even proportional equality and possesses a higher author-n law itself. The case posed by the individual of "surpassing excellence" reveals an enduring tension between the requirements of political justice and human greatness. An understanding of comprehensive virtue that takes its bearings from the necessities that govern political life does not necessarily call forth the highest human excellence. Indeed, it may even in some cases thwart its development.[22] In the present context Aristotle restricts himself to the suggestion that, even in the best circumstances, the variability of natural justice means that no existing law could foresee, much less reconcile, the full range of competing claims relevant to the determination of justice in those matters that fall within its jurisdiction.

The second wave to crash upon the shore of comprehensive justice is generated by Aristotle's consideration of the voluntary (chs. 8–9). To this point, Aristotle's analysis of justice has focused on actions rather than character. This is neither surprising nor inappropriate given the relational character of justice itself. However, Aristotle now emphasizes that law is an external standard that is, by itself, insufficient to determine whether an individual is just or not. Even more to the point, actions prescribed by law are said to be only accidentally just (5.9.1137a11–12; cf. 5.7.1135a8–11; 5.9.1136b32–34). Aristotle explains that genuinely just acts presuppose a certain disposition or state of being on the part of the one performing them (5.9.1137a8–9; 23–26).[23] Being just is not as simple as obeying the law. Moreover, knowing what justice requires in any given situation proves to be far more difficult than is generally believed. It is not sufficient to know the dictates of law, but one must also be possessed of a certain kind of wisdom (*sophos*) (5.9.1137a9–14). By turning our attention to the need for both a proper interior state and a kind of wisdom that is not easily acquired, Aristotle emphasizes the difficulty, perhaps even impossibility (5.9.1137a4–9), of genuine justice. In doing so, he continues to erode the simplistic identification of comprehensive justice with law-abidingness that provided the starting point for his consideration as a whole.

The third wave comes in the concluding discussions of equity and the possibility of psychic justice (chs. 10–11). Aristotle removes any lingering doubt about the adequacy of equating justice with law by invoking a higher standard of justice found in the equitable person. Legal justice is intrinsically defective. Although good laws mete out justice in the majority of cases, it is impossible to anticipate every situation owing to the irreducible irregularity of human affairs. Equity corrects law where law is deficient owing to its universality (*dia to katholou*) (5.10.1137b26–

27). The discussion of equity calls attention to the existence of something more primary than law. Laws have a human origin and consequently reflect the greater or lesser virtue of a legislator. The need for individuals of great wisdom and virtue does not disappear even after a regime has been founded because there is always a need to rectify law by altering, suspending, or applying it as the founders would do were they still present (5.10.1137b19–24).

The consideration of justice has now come full circle. Book V begins with an account of law as comprehensive justice; it ends with an awareness of the limits of law and the need for a higher standard of justice revealed in the actions, disposition, and wisdom of the equitable person. Unlike Plato, Aristotle stops short of identifying justice with the well-ordered soul of such an individual (cf. *Rep.* 443c–d and esp. *NE* 5.11.1138b5–14). Rather, he consistently adheres to the perspective that has shaped his discussion of justice as a whole. As we have seen, justice is essentially concerned with the public good of the political community. It is, I believe, this perspective that accounts for Aristotle's rhetorical elevation of justice as comprehensive virtue, as well as his sober appreciation for the necessarily flawed context within which the aspiration to comprehensive virtue must be grounded. The initial exaggeration of the power and scope of law emphasizes the crucial importance of law for shaping the souls of citizens. By bringing to the forefront this profound but less than conspicuous connection between law and character, Aristotle directs his readers to the highest aim and dignity of the legislative art.[24] On the other hand, his discussion of the nature of political justice and the need for a kind of virtue and wisdom beyond that which law can provide, imparts an awareness of the limits of justice as it is actually found in existing cities. The tension between the highest possibilities of law and its existential deficiencies supplies the crucible wherein political wisdom is forged.

Given the explicitly social perspective that informs Aristotle's discussion of justice, he is understandably parsimonious in his remarks about the equitable individual. Nevertheless, he includes one particularly revealing comment. Equitable persons typically take less of the goods prescribed by law than is their due, although in the process they may gain a larger share of glory or nobility (5.9.1136b20–22; cf. 5.10.1137b34–38a2). This is Aristotle's only reference to the noble (*kalos*) throughout the entire course of his consideration of justice in Book V. The concern for the noble characteristic of the magnanimous person and the concern for the common good that animates justice are not easily reconciled. Nevertheless, Aristotle suggests that one who looks to the noble is most capable of averting the unjust application of law. Aristotle's awareness of the limitations of justice in no way causes him to erode a salutary human concern for the common good. Rather, he offers a firmer basis for justice by subordinating it to something higher; the concern for justice that animates at least some equitable human beings is grounded in a preoccupation with the noble. The twin peaks of magnanimity and justice reveal the two poles in Aristotle's consideration of ethical virtue. The attempt to balance these two virtues and the various difficulties embedded in them presupposes an understanding of the nature and limits of both the noble and the just. This, in turn, requires an appreciation for a larger context including goods other than ethical virtue, in light of which the competing demands of ethical virtue can assume their proper place. Aristotle has prepared his readers for a consideration of intellectual virtue.

## THE NEED FOR INTELLECTUAL VIRTUE

Book VI can be described as the pivotal book of the *Ethics*. On the one hand, it completes Aristotle's initial presentation of ethical virtue by introducing his consideration of the relationship between ethical and intellectual excellence. Prudence, as we shall see, proves to be the third comprehensive virtue and a clarification of its essential connection to ethical virtue dominates Book VI as a whole. On the other hand, Book VI introduces several excellences in thinking that move the scope of inquiry beyond the horizon of ethical virtue. Aristotle's sparing but pointed statements about the relationship between prudence and wisdom begin to expose the limited perspective of the former and the larger horizon of inquiry opened by the latter.

Aristotle begins Book VI by returning, as promised, to the fundamental premise laid down at the outset of his consideration of ethical virtue. Virtue is distinguished from vice by deliberate action in accord with "right reason" (*orthos logos*). Aristotle had presumed an initial acceptance of this standard on the part of his readers and promised that a fuller treatment would follow (2.2.1103b31–34). He is now more forthcoming about why further consideration is necessary. The appeal to *orthos logos*, however useful and even necessary for virtuous conduct, is not very enlightening (*saphēs*) (6.1.1138b23–34). It is like telling a sick person who comes to you for help to follow the prescriptions of a medical expert. This in itself sound advice is not especially illuminating since the one suffering bodily affliction is still in the dark about what medicine or treatment to take. Further specification of the proper course of action is necessary. One must either go to the doctor or, better, learn the medical art for oneself. As Aristotle's analogy reveals, the appeal to *orthos logos* merely recasts rather than answers the original question about the mean. One can adhere to the more or less sound prescriptions of parents, teachers, and laws and still be at a loss to discover the mean for oneself. The need for further clarification is not only essential to a comprehensive treatment of ethical virtue, but is made all the more urgent given the conflicting claims of orthodox authorities and the intractable character of human experience itself.

The five intellectual virtues singled out by Aristotle are science (*epistēmē*), art (*technē*), prudence (*phronēsis*), intuitive intelligence (*nous*), and wisdom (*sophia*). The central virtue, and by far the one that receives the fullest treatment, is prudence. Aristotle's initial account takes its bearings from those who most embody this virtue. It is the mark of prudent persons that they deliberate well—not merely about what is good and advantageous in some particular area but about what is conducive to living well in general (*poia pros to eu zēn holōs*) (6.5.1140a25–28). Unlike science, prudence is the virtue of the same part of the soul that forms opinions since both prudence and opinion deal with matters that admit of being otherwise (6.5.1140b25–28; 1140a31–b2). Unlike art, which is concerned with production and results in an object distinct from the process of making it, prudence concerns the realm of action (*praxis*) where doing well (*eupraxia*) is itself the end (6.5.1140b6–7). Prudence, then, is an intellectual virtue that enables one to grasp the truth about human action. Pericles stands as its exemplar because he was generally believed to possess a capacity to discern the good both for himself and for humankind, that is, the good as it pertains to the spheres of both household management and politics (6.5.1140b7–11).

The choice of a statesman as an exemplar of prudence is not accidental. When he turns to an explanation of the relationship between prudence and political capacity (*hē politikē*),[25] Aristotle says that they are the same state (*hexis*), but they are not the same thing (6.8.1141b23–24).[26] One can express the distinction as follows. Both prudence and political capacity describe one and the same intellectual attribute, but that attribute can be looked at from different points of view. Considered as a comprehensive intellectual excellence possessed by an individual, it is called "prudence." The same disposition applied to the shared or common good of the polis is referred to as "political capacity."

Aristotle's clarification is both more compressed and more elliptical than usual. Although prudence is commonly believed to pertain most of all to the concerns of an individual, it actually embraces a broader range of activities comprising both household management and politics (6.8.1141b29–42a11).[27] Although the term *political capacity* (*politikē*) is often restricted to those carrying out the particular actions and deliberations of assemblies and law courts, it also includes a more architectonic legislative (*nomothetikē*) aspect as well (6.8.1141b24–29). In Aristotle's usage, political capacity involves both; that is, it refers to the different ways in which a constitution or regime may be arranged as well as the specific decisions, decrees, and actions that fall within a given constitutional framework. Both aspects of political capacity are part of prudence. When prudence is exercised with a view to the private good of an individual, it reveals itself as skill in household management; when it is turned toward the legislative, deliberative, or judicial aspects of communal life, it manifests itself as political capacity.

This argument qualifies, without retracting, an earlier statement to the effect that politics is the most authoritative and architectonic of the disciplines (1.2.1094a26–28). Politics is now revealed to be one part of the more comprehensive virtue of prudence.[28] The paradox, however, is readily intelligible. Politics is, in fact, the architectonic discipline, insofar as law regulates in a comprehensive and profound way the quality of political life and constitutes its supreme authority. Law, however, must be originated and excellent laws presuppose excellence on the part of those originating them. We have been prepared for this train of thought. Aristotle has already shown that the comprehensive virtue of law-abidingness is subordinate to equity. Prudence is the virtue that enables equitable individuals to correct the law in those cases where it proves deficient.[29] The architectonic good aimed at by politics presupposes an excellence it does not itself fully produce. The all-embracing and self-sufficient whole that constitutes a polis is in some sense subordinate to a part, namely, the prudent individual who, by exercising legislative skill, can both give birth to and sustain the healthy operation of a polis.[30] Although Pericles was not a founder, he is nevertheless an apt example. As a citizen of a democratic polis, Pericles was part of a larger whole; as its first citizen, the success or failure of Athens's enterprises was in some significant way determined by the degree of his prudence.[31]

Aristotle gradually works his way back to the standard of *orthos logos* with which he began, as he focuses more clearly on the relationship between prudence and ethical virtue. The prudent person is characterized by deliberative excellence (*euboulia*), a capacity described as a "kind of correctness" (*orthotēs tis*) in thinking (6.9.1142b8–9, 16). The most revealing aspect of this correctness is that it restricts deliberation to activities that enable one to arrive at a good (6.9.1142b16–22). This is different from the successful deliberation of a bad person who thereby attains something evil. The latter case evidences only cleverness (*deinotēs*), something that is presupposed by, but not identical to, prudence (6.12.1144a27–29). The crucial difference is that prudence involves some vision of the good as it appears to a virtuous person (6. 12.1144a29–37). Whereas cleverness is displayed in the correct choice of means with a view to any end, the "correctness" of the prudent person is manifest in deliberation about and specification of those activities appropriate for attaining the good of moral virtue itself. Hence, prudence is essentially dependent upon ethical virtue, without which it collapses into the morally neutral quality of cleverness.[32]

This conclusion leads to a reconsideration of ethical virtue from the point of view of prudence (6.13.1144b1–45a6). While it is possible to speak of an innate disposition toward justice, temperance, or courage— what Aristotle calls "natural virtue" (*phusikē aretē*)—this is not virtue in the full sense (*kuria aretē*). The latter requires the interior sight provided by prudence.[33] Indeed, without such interior vision, natural virtue can prove harmful. Just as a man with a powerful frame takes a particularly hard fall when he is deprived of sight, so too nascent virtue proves harmful unless it is guided by prudence. For example, young persons with an innate proclivity to act courageously are at greater risk of losing their lives on account of rashness than those lacking this good natural dispositon. Hence, Aristotle concludes that full virtue is not possible apart from prudence (6.13.1144b14–17).

The circular character of this clarification of the relationship between ethical virtue and prudence is now evident. Aristotle even calls attention to the problem when he explains that his argument has shown that it is not possible to be good apart from prudence, nor prudent apart from ethical virtue (6.13.1144b30–32).[34] It is precisely this symbiotic relationship that leads Aristotle to assert that possession of the single virtue of prudence means that one will possess all the other ethical virtues as well (6.13.1145a1–2). Prudence proves to be the third and final comprehensive virtue in Aristotle's schema and the true original of *orthos logos* itself (6.13.1144b21–24). The promised clarification of *orthos logos* with which Aristotle began Book VI turns the reader back to the sensibilities of ethically virtuous persons. This conclusion should not come as a complete surprise, inasmuch as it has been anticipated from the outset. Aristotle's original definition of ethical virtue maintained that the mean is defined by reason in the way that a prudent person defines it (2.6.1106b36–07a2). Aristotle's treatment remains faithful to this perspective; he begins and ends with an appeal to the kind of rare and comprehensive excellence found in the individual characterized by practical wisdom.

If the circular character of this argument is not altogether satisfying, it is not for that reason unintelligible. Aristotle succeeds in capturing something of the experience of all decent persons and hence clarifies, to some extent at least, the perspective of his primary audience. How exactly does ethical virtue come to be? In the best case, one begins with a natural proclivity to the virtues. But this good natural disposition requires the additional training of habitual action in order to bring the desires into harmony with the aims presented by *orthos logos*. Such guidance is initially provided by parents, teachers, and, in a decent regime, laws. However, full virtue requires more. It is only when *orthos logos* becomes a source of moral vision that emanates from within an individual, that one is truly or fully virtuous. Virtue is not merely acting in accord with the prescriptions of right reason; it is acting with or from *orthos logos* itself. It is the interior possession of *orthos logos* that Aristotle identifies with the comprehensive virtue of prudence (6.13.1144b26–28).

The value of this approach becomes apparent from even the briefest consideration of those alternatives that Aristotle rejects. He does not answer the question about what does or ought to guide the choices of decent human beings by prescribing general rules that inevitably fall short in certain circumstances. Neither does he subordinate these choices to the "shared" or "common" good of the city as it is perceived by those who rule. Instead, the primary desideratum of the prudent person retains the form of a question: How will I be good in this situation? What would be the noble course of action? By avoiding dangerously simplistic sources of guidance, and without stepping beyond the horizon of moral virtue itself, Aristotle encourages decent persons to demand of themselves the highest excellence of which they are capable.

On the other hand, the circular character of Aristotle's account points to the limits of the horizon within which the virtuous understand themselves and, as a consequence, the need for something more.[35] Insofar as prudence is identified with *orthos logos*, it presupposes, rather than critically assesses, the intuitive perceptions of morally decent persons. This problem may underlie Aristotle's assertion that prudence belongs to the part of the soul that forms opinions (6.5.1140b25–30; 6.13.1144b14–17). Virtuous persons necessarily act on the basis of things that they do not know but only opine. However necessary this may be for the development of ethical virtue, it is, in Aristotle's estimation, not especially enlightening (recall 6.1.1138b25–34). The serious and sustained quest for knowledge that culminates in wisdom requires a ground both firmer and more expansive than the cultivated soil in which ethical virtue puts down its deepest roots.

## THE COMPETING CLAIMS OF PRUDENCE AND WISDOM

Aristotle's account of the relationship between ethical virtue and prudence is punctuated by brief but revealing considerations of the relationship between prudence and wisdom. In the course of his discussion of the hierarchy of intellectual virtues, he unambiguously affirms that at the peak of that hierarchy stands wisdom (*sophia*). Wisdom is the most exact (*akribestatē*) form of scientific knowledge. It refers to excellence in not only one area or endeavor but rather to "general" or "complete" intellectual excellence (*holēs, ou kata meros*). The wise person knows not only what is derived from the first principles of science but also grasps the truth about the principles themselves. Hence, wisdom is intelligence (*nous*) plus scientific knowledge (*epistēmē*), a "science of the most honored things with, as it were, intelligence as its head or capstone" (6.7.1141a9–20). Based on this description, it would be strange to suppose that either prudence or politics is the most serious (*spoudaiotatē*) form of knowing, inasmuch as the best thing in the universe is not a human being (6.7.1141a20–22).[36]

Aristotle sharpens this conclusion about the relative standing of prudence, politics, and wisdom by matching his earlier exemplar of prudence with corresponding exemplars of wisdom. Anaxagoras and Thales were generally thought to possess extraordinary, marvelous, difficult, and even godlike knowledge, but were not deemed prudent because they were ignorant of the things that are good for human beings (6.7.1141b3–9). They stand in sharp contrast to Pericles whose claim to practical wisdom derived precisely from his capacity to discern what was good for himself and for his fellow citizens (6.5.1140b7–11). Practical and theoretical wisdom are the only two intellectual virtues to be personified in Book VI. Aristotle's use of offsetting models for the two peaks of intellectual virtue subtly but effectively introduces readers to a rivalry between the competing demands and claims of moral-political and philosophic excellence.

Aristotle frames the contest in an extreme way by choosing two philosophers who, according to the account provided here, appear to be utterly indifferent to the more urgent and pervasive human concern with human affairs.[37] An initial effect of this characterization is to suggest the unlikeness of theoretical and practical wisdom, an unlikeness that in some way defuses the potential for conflict by suggesting that each has little to do with the other. A further consequence of the apparent remoteness of theoretical wisdom from the more immediate world of human experience is that it recognizes, to some extent at least, the respectability of the more pervasive opinion that prudence ought to be regarded as the pinnacle of human wisdom. Is it not true that, as human beings and citizens, we must necessarily and in the first place be concerned with specifically human affairs? It is this eminently practical viewpoint that explains why outstanding statesmen such as Pericles are held in greater esteem than natural philosophers such as Anaxagoras and Thales.

Aristotle acknowledges but resists the force of this opinion by pointing to an apparent paradox. It would be strange, he writes, if prudence, which is inferior to wisdom, should possess greater authority (*kuriōtera*) than wisdom (6.12.1143b33–34). Aristotle's concise but trenchant responses to this paradox come in three parts. He defends the usefulness of wisdom by maintaining that it does, in fact, produce an effect of immediate and compelling interest for human beings.

> Wisdom produces happiness, not in the way that medical art produces health, but in the way that healthiness produces health. Being a part of virtue as a whole, its possession, or rather its activity, makes a person happy. (6.12.1144a3–6)

This first part of Aristotle's response is striking. The issue of happiness that dominated Book I as the first principle and final end of human activity reenters the discussion only at this point. It comes at the very end of Aristotle's discussion of ethical virtue and is presented as the result, not of ethical virtue or of prudence, but of wisdom. Although wisdom is said to be a part of virtue as a whole, Aristotle's analogy emphasizes the intrinsic connection between the activity of wisdom and happiness.

What then is the relationship between prudence and happiness? Although Aristotle's thematic treatment of happiness must await his discussion in Book X, his return to the medical analogy at the end of Book VI provides the second part of his response to the original paradox.[38] Aristotle explains:

> Prudence does not have authority over wisdom or the better part of the soul any more than the medical art has authority over health. For the medical art does not control health but looks at how it comes to be; hence, it issues orders for the sake of health, but not to health. (6.13.1145a6–9)

Aristotle likens wisdom to health and prudence to medical skill. Just as the art of medicine attempts to secure health for beings subject to the contingencies of bodily existence, prudence attempts to arrange the varied circumstances of political life so as to insure an optimum of both psychic and physical health for citizens. Given Aristotle's comparison of healthiness to happiness in the first part of the analogy, the extension of the metaphor in this passage implies the existence of an instrumental relationship between prudence and happiness. Although prudence is unable to control happiness, it is useful, indeed indispensable, in providing the conditions for its enjoyment by the wise.[39]

Aristotle's third and concluding response to the paradox returns in an explicit way to the political importance of prudence that had given rise to its initial claim to possess greater authority than theoretical wisdom. To suppose that prudence is more authoritative than wisdom "is like saying that politics rules the gods because it gives orders about everything in the polis" (6.13.1145a10–11). Although politics issues decrees about religious sacrifices and festivals, it is ludicrous to think that the city is able to rule the very gods to whom it turns to secure its welfare. Similarly, although politics necessarily regulates the public activities of the wise, it would be wrong to think that it oversees their godlike wisdom or even that such wisdom is circumscribed by the necessities that govern political life. Politics gives orders about everything in the city, but its authority cannot adequately encompass those whose wisdom in some way transcends the horizon of concerns proper to politics itself.

The reverence accorded to Pericles by popular opinion stems from the importance of prudence for political life. From the point of view of the city, the political wisdom of Pericles seems far more important than the philosophic wisdom of Anaxagoras or Thales. Despite the marvelous character of such knowledge, philosophic neglect of human affairs renders Anaxagoras and Thales imprudent and that imprudence diminishes their stature as wise human beings. The plausibility of Aristotle's argument on behalf of wisdom does not, however, rest on the authority of Anaxagoras or Thales. Between the two extremes of philosophers without prudence and statesmen without philosophy stands an unarticulated middle ground occupied by Aristotle himself. *Political* philosophy is an activity that is neither indifferent to nor walled in by the vicissitudes of political life. This middle position is not yet explicitly mentioned by Aristotle, but his sympathetic clarification of ethical virtue in Books II–V and judicious treatment of prudence in Book VI have amply demonstrated it. Aristotle's claim for the greater authority of theoretical wisdom gains in credibility by the prudential concern that he exercises on behalf of those virtues most conducive to the welfare of the city.

We are now in a better position to appreciate the sense in which Book VI is the pivotal book of the *Ethics*. It both completes Aristotle's treatment of the ethical virtues as desirable in themselves and, hence, as constituting the proper end of human action, and reveals the existence of a broader horizon within which ethical virtue can be regarded as a means to another end. The comprehensive virtue of prudence contributes to the emergence of the only activity explicitly identified with happiness. The suggestion that ethical virtue is a means to some further end necessarily calls into question the teaching that it is an end in itself. If the virtues are themselves means, or at least can be so understood by the wise, in what sense is it possible to maintain that the noble provides a sufficient standard for the best human life? By raising this question in a discrete manner in Book VI, Aristotle prepares the way for his most explicit presentation of the radical alternative to the life of the *kalos k'agathos* in Book VII.

# CHAPTER THREE

# A New Beginning: Incontinence and Pleasure, Book VII

## THE NEW HORIZON: PUZZLE AND DISCOVERY

Book VII opens with an announcement of a new beginning. The preceding six books have injected unprecedented clarity into the phenomena of ethical virtue, given special attention to its guiding principle, and returned to the issue of happiness with which the study began. Although the consideration of ethical virtue is complete by the end of Book VI, the suggestive and undeveloped remarks about wisdom with which this book concludes point to the need for further investigation.

Aristotle introduces his new beginning with the assertion that the things pertaining to character ( *ta ēthē* ) can be considered from three different points of view, each of which is delimited by a pair of opposites: (1) virtue and vice, (2) continence and incontinence,[1] and (3) the divine and the brutish. This threefold classification introduces two new perspectives, each of which needs to be distinguished from the primary categories of virtue and vice that provide the initial framework for the treatise.

The first of the new categories, continence and incontinence, supplies the theme for the first part of Book VII (chs.1–10). This new classification is neither identical to, nor different in kind from, that provided by virtue and vice (7.1.1145a36–45b2). It is made necessary by the loftiness of the account of ethical excellence. The high tone of this treatment was especially evident in Aristotle's presentation of the three peak virtues considered in the previous chapter. At their best, virtuous persons embody what is great in every virtue, possess perfect virtue toward others, and act from an interior principle of right reason that embraces all the ethical virtues. Although Aristotle has shaded his analysis with some indication of the problems involved in the very notion of comprehensive virtue, he now turns as a matter of practical necessity to a thematic consideration of the experience of those who fail to reach this lofty summit. Judged from the point of view of ethical virtue, the treatment of continence and incontinence appears to be a lower but necessary concession to those who are unable to sustain its rigorous and inclusive demands.

The second new mode of classification further broadens the horizon of inquiry by adverting to conditions lower than vice and higher than virtue. Whereas the former brutish state sinks below the standard of ethical behavior, the latter heroic or godlike condition exceeds it.[2] The elaboration of this new classification is, however, puzzling. Whereas the subsequent consideration explicitly addresses the issue of brutishness, there is no comparable account of heroic or surpassing human excellence.[3] Either Aristotle fails to provide the consideration that he anticipates here or he offers it in an unanticipated way. I will attempt to show that the concern for an excellence that surpasses ethical virtue, far from dropping out of his consideration, furnishes the unifying theme for the remainder of the *Ethics* (Bks. VII–X). Each of the thematic discussions that follow upon Aristotle's treatment of incontinence—pleasure, friendship, and happiness—point to a kind of excellence that in some way transcends the horizon of moral virtue. We should note, however, that these topics receive very different treatments in the books that follow, differences that derive from the pedagogical and rhetorical structure that informs the treatise as a whole.

It is important to emphasize that the new account of "matters pertaining to character" does not replace or obviate the first account. Rather, Aristotle overlays the primary categories of virtue and vice with two new points of view: He considers a standard of moral seriousness that is lower and more accessible than the lofty target by which he initially set the sights of his readers, while, at the same time, broadening the scope of inquiry to include the rare but revealing conditions of human beings who border on the bestial and the divine.

Aristotle's second beginning in Book VII is appropriately accompanied by a statement about method (7.1.1145b2–7). It is first necessary to set out the appearances (*phainomena*) and then go through the various puzzles or difficulties (*aporiai*) embedded in them.[4] After attempting to remove as many of the discrepancies and contradictions as possible, the residuum of decent opinion (*endoxa*) left standing will have been made sufficiently clear. Aristotle records a variety of opinions about continence and incontinence (7.1.1145b8–20), brings to light six problems entangled in those opinions (7.2.1145b21–46b8), and then attempts to disentangle them (7.3.1146b8–52a36). The unraveling of such a puzzle is, he explains, a discovery (7.2.1146b7–8). Although Aristotle specifies six difficulties that stand in need of clarification, his own consideration of them does not follow the expected order. The problems are instead divided into two groups (7.3.1146b8–14). It is first necessary to consider the Socratic paradox: Do incontinent persons have knowledge or not, and in what sense might they have it (ch. 3)? In the second place, Aristotle takes up the remaining problems in such a way as to delimit the nature and scope of continence and incontinence as well as the relationship of these states to virtue and vice (chs. 4–10). The consideration that follows takes its bearings from this twofold division.[5]

Commentators often uncritically assimilate Aristotle's statement of method in Book VII to his treatise as a whole, an assimilation that blunts the sharp edge of his stated intention to begin anew. Unlike the first beginning, Book VII neither stresses the necessarily imprecise character of ethical inquiry, nor speaks of the need to ascertain the first principles of ethics from the experience provided by a decent upbringing. As will soon become clear, Aristotle's new beginning takes its bearings from a philosophic problem, specifically, a conflict between the widespread view that human beings sometimes act in ways they know to be wrong and a Socratic teaching that denies this possibility. By formulating puzzles and seeking to elicit discoveries, students are introduced to the more explicitly philosophical, even Socratic, mode of inquiry that characterizes this book as a whole.

The most pervasive scholarly explanation for this shift in perspective is drawn from the fact that Book VII is one of the books common to both the *Nicomachean* and *Eudemian Ethics*. The prevailing view is that the *Eudemian* version, unlike the *Nicomachean* one, was addressed to those who were philosophically inclined, something that is preserved in the shared Book VII. I do not so much disagree with this view as find it inadequate as an explanation. My own interpretation attempts to elucidate the underlying coherence of the *Nicomachean Ethics* as it now stands. I am less interested in the relationship between the two versions of the *Ethics* (an important question in its own right), and far more interested in the ways in which the various parts of the *Nicomachean Ethics* fit together. This approach leads me to take issue with, or at least qualify, a scholarly differentiation of audiences that is currently gaining ground; namely, that the *Eudemian Ethics* is addressed primarily to philosophers and the *Nicomachean Ethics* to future politicians. Whatever may be true of the *Eudemian Ethics*, I dispute the restriction of the intended audience of the *Nicomachean Ethics* to potential politicians, in large measure because such a view dismisses or at least minimizes the impact of Book VII on this question. Instead of ruling out a priori the evidence provided by this part of the treatise because it is regarded as a vestige of an earlier (as most scholars believe) *Eudemian* account, investigation into the possible unity of the *Nicomachean Ethics* requires that Book VII be given its proper weight in determining the intended audience of the work as a whole. This, in turn, leads to the novel thesis argued here; namely, that shifts in perspective within the ten books of the *Nicomachean Ethics* are best explained by positing the existence of a dual audience comprised of both philosophers and nonphilosophers. In keeping with this hypothesis, the following analysis is especially attentive to the pedagogical and rhetorical implications of a change in vantage point that receives its sharpest and most sustained development only at this juncture in Aristotle's study.

INCONTINENCE: CLARIFYING SOCRATES' ETHICAL PARADOX

The first of the puzzles identified by Aristotle raises a question about the kind of "right conception" (*pōs hupolambanōn orthōs*) characteristic of those believed to act incontinently (7.2.1145b21–46a9).[6] The problem is focused most sharply by Socrates who thought that it would be strange if, while knowledge was present, something else could overpower it and drag it around like a slave (7.2.1145b23–24). In fact, he used to combat this view altogether. Socrates maintained that no one acts contrary to what is best while knowing that what one is doing is bad; actions falling short of goodness are due instead to ignorance. The most jarring aspect of this Socratic teaching is that it denies the existence of incontinence (7.2.1145b25–27), and in so doing raises a question about the nature and extent of moral culpability.[7] Aristotle's formulation of the puzzle expresses sympathy for those who experience Socrates' outlandish position on such an important matter with something like frustrated indignation. The Socratic view, Aristotle asserts, is clearly at odds with things that appear most manifest (*tois phainomenois enargōs*) (7.2.1145b27–28).[8]

Aristotle's attempt to unravel the first puzzle about the status of knowing is divided into a preface and four difficult and abbreviated arguments leading to a final evaluation (7.3.1146b24–47b19).[9] Commentators generally agree that the first three arguments are "dialectical" or "logical" (*logikōs*) and that the fourth is "natural" or "physical" (*phusikōs*).[10] Although Aristotle does not always apply the distinction sharply, for the most part *logikōs* arguments employ principles or distinctions that pertain to many different subjects, whereas a *phusikōs* explanation treats a topic in terms of its own proper and distinct principles, at least when the matter falls within the sphere of natural science.[11] It is sufficient for our purposes to summarize the conclusions of each of these arguments, noting especially their bearing on the problem raised by Socrates.

The first argument differentiates two kinds of knowing by making use of Aristotle's far-reaching distinction between potential (*dunamis*) and actualization (*energeia*). He maintains that it would not be surprising if people were to act against knowledge that they possessed but were not currently using, although it would be strange if they acted against knowledge while they were actively beholding (*theōrounta*) it. Aristotle's second argument adds greater technical precision to his first by deploying the doctrine of the practical syllogism. Two kinds of premises, universal and particular, are involved in knowing how to act. Aristotle observes that it would not be strange to act against knowledge of both universal and particular premises if, in a specific case, one had considered only the universal and not the particular. For example, one might know that dry food is healthy for a human being, that one is a human being, and even that food of a certain kind is dry, but still fail to realize that the food before one was of that sort. Aristotle adds, however, that it would be astonishing (*thaumastos*) if the individual in question acted contrary to knowledge in which both universal and particular propositions were apprehended as concrete particulars.

Both of these arguments make use of the distinction between potential and actualization to explain how or in what sense persons undertaking bad actions could act against a knowledge that they nevertheless possess. On this account, it is possible for an individual to have a right conception or even a true syllogism, but in each case an important aspect of that conception or syllogism is inactive such that the incontinent person is ignorant at the time of action. The deed may be regretted and one may even be responsible for one's ignorance, but at the moment of action, the knowledge that what one is doing is wrong is only potentially, not actively, present. Aristotle's next two arguments begin to explain how the knowledge in question might come to be absent. It should be noted, however, that Aristotle's attempt to preserve the commonsense view of incontinence (acting against what one correctly conceives to be wrong) does not refute the Socratic position. According to the arguments provided so far, incontinent persons do not act against what they actually know to be wrong; rather, they act in ignorance of knowledge that is possessed in potential only.

In his third argument, Aristotle introduces another way in which one can both have and not have knowledge by pointing to the condition of those who are asleep, mad, or drunk. Aristotle explains that persons under the influence of "feeling" or "emotion" (*pathos*) are in the same state. Strong passions, such as anger and sexual desire, can alter both bodily and mental states and, in extreme cases, even cause madness. Incontinent persons possess knowledge in the same way as those who are asleep, drunk, or mad; their reaction to feelings and, more specifically, the pleasures associated with them, prevents the relevant knowledge from being actualized at the time the deed is being undertaken.[12] Moreover, using the language of knowledge, even at the crucial moment, is no proof that it is really present. Aristotle compares the situation to young students who correctly recite what they have learned without understanding the significance of what they are saying because the learning at issue has not yet "grown into them" (*sumphuēnai*) (7.3.1147a22). Incontinent persons fail in the same way. Even if they were to express correctly the principle they are at that moment violating, it does not count as genuine knowledge since the knowledge in question has not yet become part of their nature.

Aristotle's final argument elaborates this explanation from the viewpoint of natural philosophy (*phusikōs*). The argument begins with a recapitulation and development of the doctrine of the practical syllogism and concludes with a description of the physiological state in which rational control is temporarily overcome by emotion or pleasure, a state comparable to that produced by drunkenness or sleep. Notwithstanding the textual difficulties involved in this compressed argument, there is no difficulty in recognizing Aristotle's conclusion. One reacting to the influence of emotion or pleasure either does not possess knowledge or possesses it in a defective way, much like a drunken man who repeats the sound moral maxims of Empedocles without allowing them to affect his behavior in the least (7.3.1147b9–12). Aristotle's striking conclusion makes explicit the identity of the major interlocutor in his treatment of incontinence: "We seem to be led to the position that Socrates sought to establish—it is not knowledge in the authoritative sense (*kuriōs epistēmē*) that is overcome in an incontinent act, nor is such knowledge dragged around by emotion" (7.3.1147b14–17).

For all the difficulty of Aristotle's particular arguments in this section, their overall effect is clear. Aristotle argues that it is in fact possible to act against some conception of right. In opposition to the Socratic paradox, Aristotle maintains that incontinence both exists and is intelligible, and will go on in subsequent chapters to delineate with greater precision its nature and scope. However, Aristotle's initial consideration also and especially points to a kind of knowing that cannot be overcome by emotion. While disagreeing with Socrates in such a way as to shed light on an all too familiar aspect of human experience, Aristotle begins to suggest the proper way to understand a much less familiar Socratic maxim by pointing to the existence of a rare and authoritative kind of knowledge that was the object of Socratic investigation. The particular arguments that Aristotle makes in this section address the question of moral goodness from the perspective of both dialectic and natural philosophy. Within this broader horizon of inquiry, Aristotle attempts to move his readers from an initial frustration with the patently outlandish character of Socratic inquiry to some appreciation for the less than obvious truth to which that inquiry was devoted. In effect, Aristotle's justification of the Socratic paradox provides his readers with a greater appreciation for the requirements of knowledge in a strict sense, that is, the kind of authoritative knowledge sought by the wise (see 6.7.1141a16–20 and 6.13.1145a6–11).

## INCONTINENCE: PRESERVING DECENT OPINION

Although Aristotle vindicates Socrates' claim about the unassailable character of a certain kind of knowledge, he disagrees with the radical conclusion of the Socratic position. Socrates' denial of incontinence may follow with theoretical force from his investigations, but for Aristotle, his dialectical conclusion is refuted by the very pervasiveness of the phenomenon it seeks to deny. The remainder of Aristotle's discussion of incontinence attempts to clarify its nature and scope by being especially attentive to the kinds of ignorance involved in voluntary wrongdoing. The first part (chs. 4–10) differentiates continence and incontinence from similar but distinct states of virtue and vice by providing a taxonomy of different states of character from the point of view of incontinence. The second part of Aristotle's treatment (chs. 11–14) is an initial thematic consideration of pleasure that is precipitated by the centrality of pleasure in the analysis of incontinence.[13]

Aristotle's account of incontinence turns on the place and importance of pleasure in decision making. He begins with an initial distinction between necessary pleasures associated with the activities of the body (food, drink, sex) and pleasures that are not necessary, in the sense that physical species-sustaining activities are, but are nevertheless desirable in themselves (7.4.1147b23–31; 1148a22–27). Within this second category, some pleasures are intrinsically desirable (e.g., contemplation and virtue), others become so by accident or perversion (e.g., convalescence and cannibalism), and still others are "intermediate" (*metaxu*), being neither intrinsically good nor intrinsically bad (e.g., material goods, wealth, victory, and honor). Strictly speaking, incontinence refers to the first category of necessary bodily pleasures, although it is possible to speak of incontinence in a qualified sense with respect to the intermediate pleasures as well. Both the lower case of pleasures enjoyed by bestial or diseased dispositions and the intrinsically desirable pleasures, about which Aristotle will have more to say in subsequent discussions, fall outside the sphere of continence and incontinence in its primary meaning.

What then is the relationship between incontinence and profligacy (*akolasia*) since both pertain to bodily pleasures, specifically those involving touch and taste? Although it is impossible to distinguish them on the basis of their outward appearance, Aristotle explains that the essential difference lies in the presence or absence of inner conflict in the process of making and evaluating decisions. Incontinent persons experience conflict between right principle (*orthos logos*) and feeling (*pathos*) or appetite (*epithumia*) (7.8.1151a20–24). Their reaction to pleasure or the prospect of pleasure is such that they fail to act on the basis of right reason without, however, being persuaded that they ought to pursue such pleasures in an unrestrained way. Profligate persons, on the other hand, experience no inner conflict. Not only do they pursue available bodily pleasures, but they are also convinced that they ought to do so (7.8.1151a11–14). Hence, incontinence forms a kind of halfway house. Incontinent persons are not simply bad since the first principles of decent action have not been obliterated by their reactions to pleasure. However, neither can they be considered good since the lure of pleasure has eroded their character to the point where they fail to determine their actions on the basis of those decent principles to which they give intellectual assent. The incontinent person is compared by Aristotle to a city with good laws but whose citizens fail to keep them. The profligate, by contrast, is like a city whose citizens abide by the laws but whose laws are bad (7.10.1152a19–24).

Continent and temperate persons are likewise indistinguishable judged from the standpoint of deeds, since neither the continent nor the temperate act against right principle on account of bodily pleasure. However, temperate persons are so constituted as to take no pleasure in anything contrary to *orthos logos*, whereas continent persons are pulled by base desires (*phaulas epithumias*), and so feel the tug of those pleasures they successfully resist (7.9.1151b35–52a3). Most people fall somewhere between the continent and the incontinent person (7. 10.1152a25–27). Correct principle does not successfully vanquish the seductive power of all inappropriate bodily pleasures, but neither is it compelled to accept unconditional surrender. Indeed, given the difficulty of becoming fully temperate, that is, of finding pleasure in nothing contrary to right principle, the sphere of continence and incontinence describes not only those in the process of developing the virtue of temperance but very likely the condition of most human beings. The war between right principle and pleasure continues unabated with victories on both sides of the field.

Aristotle also gives considerable attention to incontinence in a qualified sense, the case in which, for example, someone is said to be incontinent with respect to spiritedness, honor, or gain (7.4.1148b11–14). Although these activities and the intermediate pleasures that accompany them are good in themselves, the enjoyment of them can be excessive or deficient. Such activities can also be enjoyed in the wrong way or with an improper sense of priorities. Aristotle's analysis of incontinence in a qualified sense extends the sphere of continent and incontinent behavior in such a way as to encompass ethical states in addition to temperance and profligacy. The particular examples given here—incontinence with respect to spiritedness, honor, and gain—suggest parallel accounts for the treatment of courage, mildness, proper ambition, magnanimity, justice, generosity, and magnificence.

Nevertheless, Aristotle's analysis makes incontinence in the strict sense the paradigmatic case. Perhaps this is because it is in the case of necessary bodily activities that the influence of pleasure in the determination of human action is most apparent, whereas one might not initially think of a situation involving spiritedness, honor, or gain in this way.[14] As Aristotle has made clear in the first part of his treatise, it is both sensible and intelligible to understand a grasping individual in terms of excessive preoccupation with gain and the overambitious individual as suffering from excessive attachment to honor. The new, more Socratic thought that Aristotle is now contending with, is that all such attachments can be understood in light of the broader, simpler, and unambiguously natural category of pleasure. In each case, it is the powerful appeal of pleasure, albeit of different kinds, that eclipses right principle in the action that is undertaken. Aristotle is still dealing with the consequences of the deceptively penetrating Socratic thesis that ignorance of true pleasure accounts for much of human behavior (*Protag.* 351c–61c).

Aristotle counters this view by insisting that the failure of incontinent persons is not merely a failure of knowledge; it also involves character. The tendency to give pleasure more weight than it ought to possess may stem from actual ignorance of potential knowledge, but over time the habitual slide toward pleasure shapes character and so creates a condition in which one is less likely to resist its charms on the basis of principles that one knows or believes to be right. For Aristotle, this is a culpable failure in knowledge or, at least, correct opinion. Such a person is not simply bad because their deliberation is decent (7.10.1152a16–18), something reflected in the regret they feel for what they have done. Yet they are blameworthy because they have developed a character in which their reaction to pleasure has too much influence in the determination of their actions. Aristotle will have considerably more to say about the place and importance of pleasure in the thematic treatments of it that follow. In the present context, he restricts himself to a delicate reference to Neoptolemus, a character in Sophocles' *Philoctetes* (7.9. 1151b17–22). Neoptolemus was led by pleasure to abandon a resolution that he had made with Odysseus. However, Neoptolemus's action was not blameworthy because the pleasure that caused him to withdraw from Odysseus's scheme was the noble pleasure that he took in speaking the truth. Aristotle educes a suggestive and as yet undeveloped moral: Neoptolemus's praiseworthy act reveals that not everyone whose conduct is guided by pleasure is profligate, base, or incontinent.

Aristotle distinguishes the various states of voluntary wrongdoing (incontinence, profligacy, baseness) from a lower brutish condition that could only be described as incontinence in the most attenuated sense. In point of fact, however, this condition is neither incontinent nor profligate for in this case the deliberative capacity is not corrupt; it is altogether absent (7.7.1151a1–3). Brutish persons are not responsible agents because they lack the capacity to know what they are doing. Although extreme cases of incontinence or profligacy may resemble the actions of brutish persons, the cases are as different from one another as are the actions of lower animals in comparison to specifically human behavior. Beastlike conduct in human beings is more horrible than vice, although it is less bad; it may be repulsive and even dangerous, but it is not blameworthy. Like Socrates, Aristotle recognizes a state in which one fails to do the good because of *in*voluntary ignorance. However, unlike Socrates, Aristotle restricts this phenomena to rare cases that lie on the borders of human nature.

It is important to note that Aristotle differentiates different types of incontinence (7.7.1150b19–28). Whereas incontinence of weakness (*astheneia*) is characterized by the breaking of a deliberate resolution, incontinence of impetuousness (*propeteia*) characterizes those who forego deliberation altogether. The two temperaments most susceptible to this second form of incontinence are the quick tempered and the "ardent" or "intense" (*melancholikos*).[15] It is this latter disposition that is of greatest interest, given what Aristotle says about it elsewhere. The *melancholikos* may be especially susceptible to incontinence, yet this same disposition also characterizes those who become in some way extraordinary, particularly with respect to intellectual virtue. The disposition is analyzed in the *Problems* where Empedocles, Plato, and Socrates, among others, are given as examples.[16]

Aristotle prefaces his consideration of pleasure by returning in an enigmatic way to the case of the *melancholikos* (7.10.1152a27–33). He seems to maintain two different and conflicting positions. He asserts that the incontinence of the *melancholikos* is more easily cured than the kind of incontinence that characterizes those who deliberate (i.e., an incontinence of weakness according to Aristotle's earlier classification), but then immediately goes on to say that incontinence based on habit or upbringing is more easily cured than incontinence based on nature. The perplexity stems from the fact that the disposition of the *melancholikos* is emphatically the result of nature, not habit or upbringing.[17] Each of Aristotle's two concluding statements seems to refute the other.

Is there a way to understand this apparent contradiction? From one point of view, an incontinence of weakness based on bad habits is easier to cure because, as Aristotle has already indicated, regret can lead one to change those habits. Preservation of right principle together with discontent concerning one's lack of resolve, provide a basis for the desired change. On the other hand, what are we to make of Aristotle's puzzling assertion that the natural proclivity to incontinence characteristic of the *melancholikos* might be more easily curable than an incontinence based on habit? The answer, I believe, lies in the treatment of pleasure that follows. For the moment I offer only the following provocative suggestion: The "cure" for those moved by the intense desires of the *melancholikos* does not require their removal or change; rather, it presupposes their fulfillment. Aristotle has at this point sufficiently prepared his readers, particularly the more thoughtful among them, for a thematic discussion of pleasure.

## PLEASURE AND POLITICAL PHILOSOPHY

One of the most puzzling features of the *Ethics* is that it includes two distinct treatments of pleasure: Book VII, 11–14 and Book X, 1–5. Neither discussion mentions the other and, although the issues and arguments presented in each account overlap, the differences between the texts are serious enough to raise questions about their compatibility.

A mountain of modern scholarship has been generated in the effort to address the problems posed by this part of the treatise. At the risk of oversimplifying, it is possible to extract two authors who best frame the debate. A. J. Festugière argues that the double treatment of pleasure in the *Ethics* repeats too much to belong to the same work and, by the same argument, must be regarded as the work of the same author. He maintains that the second account in Book X is Aristotle's more mature and definitive treatment of pleasure, whereas his first one in Book VII was originally part of the earlier *Eudemian* version and was only later transferred to the *Nicomachean Ethics*.[18] Since the appearance of Festugière's study, the tendency among scholars has been to play down the differences in the two accounts of pleasure, viewing them instead as different stages in Aristotle's effort to develop a single, unified teaching on this subject.[19]

This view has been challenged by G. E. L. Owen, who argues that Aristotle's treatment of pleasure in Book VII cannot be adequately understood as a rough version of his more polished account in Book X.[20] He maintains that each inquiry possesses a teaching of its own and the attempt to harmonize, or at least minimize, the differences that distinguish them does not do justice to the text. Owen observes that Aristotle's discussion in Book VII raises a question about the nature of pleasure itself, an issue that is not his primary concern in Book X.[21] He contends that the discrepancies in these two accounts result from the attempt to deal with different aspects of the problem of pleasure. If the two studies have traditionally been considered too divergent to be compatible, Owen argues that they are too divergent to be *in*compatible.[22]

Although the studies of Festugière and Owen are indispensable for understanding the issues involved in Aristotle's dual treatment of pleasure, I hope to show that attentiveness to the immediate contexts and particular purposes of these discussions, what can generally be called the political character of Aristotle's treatment, yields a richer understanding of the text as it now stands.

Aristotle begins his discussion of pleasure in Book VII by asserting that such an inquiry is proper to political philosophy. This is, in fact, his only explicit reference to political philosophy in the *Ethics* and it is worth quoting in full.

> It also belongs to the political philosopher to study (*theōrēsai*) pleasure and pain; for he is the master craftsman (*architektōn*) of the end to which we look when we call each thing good or bad in an unqualified sense. (7.11.1152b1–3)

At least two points should be noted about this introduction. The first concerns Aristotle's decision to offer a thematic treatment of pleasure. Pleasure is not, of course, a new subject in the *Ethics*. As we have already observed, after an initial dismissal of the life devoted to pleasure in Book I, the topic was reintroduced because of its importance for the development of character. What is new, however, is that Aristotle now recommends pleasure as something worthy of serious philosophic study in its own right. This recommendation furnishes a starting point for the thesis argued here: The account of pleasure in Book VII is addressed especially to philosophers or at least potential philosophers, in contrast to earlier and later considerations where the treatment of pleasure is subordinated to the moral-political horizon that dominates the *Ethics* as a whole.

Secondly, the introduction of the theme of pleasure in Book VII completes an argument that has been gradually unfolding since Book I. Aristotle began the *Ethics* by emphasizing the dignity of politics (*politikē*), asserting that it is the most authoritative and architectonic of the disciplines (1.2.1094a26–28). In Book VI, he further specified that the architectonic element within politics is the art or science of legislation (*nomothetikē*), and that popular opinion identifies this and every aspect of political capacity with those most directly involved in the political arena (6.8.1141b23–29). As we have seen, this is particularly true of a prudent statesman such as Pericles who, because of his understanding of human affairs, was held in higher esteem than Anaxagoras or Thales despite the lofty character of their wisdom. It is only at this point in his study that Aristotle, speaking in his own name, reveals that the master craftsman of politics is not the statesman, but the political philosopher. This completes his earlier contrast between statesmen without wisdom and philosophers without prudence. The hitherto unarticulated middle ground of political philosophy occupied by Aristotle himself is for the first time explicitly brought into the study. Contrary to a more pervasive view, it is not the statesman but the political philosopher who in some, as yet unspecified, way determines the standard of human excellence itself.[23]

The treatment of pleasure in Book VII can be divided into three major parts. After listing three conspicuous opinions about pleasure and the arguments that support them, Aristotle begins his response by taking issue with the view that no pleasure is a good (7.12–13.1152b25–53b7). The second and central section takes up the general view that pleasure cannot be the supreme good (7.13.1153b7–54a7). He concludes with a consideration of bodily pleasure that is primarily directed against the view that most pleasures are base (7.14.1154a8–54b34).

## PLEASURE AS END

The first section is comprised of three general arguments that address different meanings of the good, accidental as opposed to essential pleasures, and pleasure as activity and end. The first argument distinguishes two different meanings of the word *good*: that which is good without qualification and that which is good for someone (7.12.1152b25–33). Aristotle observes that, even if one were correct in asserting that no pleasure is simply good, it does not follow from this that pleasure is not good for some particular individual. Further, even those pleasures considered bad for a particular individual may at certain times be good. To illustrate with an example from the *Politics*, it is not enough for a good trainer to know the proper amount of exercise and diet for an Olympian athlete, since the same prescription would harm someone with lesser physical abilities, or even the Olympian athlete himself if he were recovering from an injury (*Pol.* 4.1.1288b10–21). So too, in an inquiry given over to the human good, any general teaching about human happiness must take into account the specific and inevitably different capacities of its addressees. Aristotle's consideration in Book VII offers readers the opportunity to test their capacities by inviting them to study the question of pleasure as political philosophers.

The core of the second argument (7.12.1152b33–53a7) is based on the distinction between "restorative pleasures" that are only accidentally pleasant, and those pleasures that can be experienced without pain or desire because they are pleasant in an unqualified sense. Accidental or restorative pleasures are "in process" (*genesis*) or, more precisely, are associated with a process of becoming since they lead to the perfection of our natural state. The pleasure of eating, for example, falls into this category. The process is experienced as pleasurable because it brings about a healthy natural condition. This distinction is used to oppose the view that pleasures are not good because they are motivated by pain or desire, which implies deficiency (in this example, hunger). Aristotle concludes that although restorative pleasures are only accidentally pleasant, some pleasures do not fall into this category and so need not be excluded from the good.

In the present context, the single example of pleasure not belonging to this first category is contemplation (7.12.1152b36–53a2). This kind of pleasure cannot be understood as a "process" or "becoming" because it is not born of deficiency nor does it "restore" us to our normal condition; rather, it is the activity of a healthy or fully developed nature. Aristotle's example begins to clarify his initial claim that the philosopher in some sense provides the fundamental standard for human life by anticipating a teaching that he will make explicit only in the concluding book of his study. The truly pleasant activity of contemplation provides the measure against which other goods are to be evaluated.

The third general argument in this section (7.12.1153a7–17) takes issue with the view that pleasure, because it is a "becoming," cannot be a good that possesses the status of an "end." However, not all pleasures are processes or incidental to them. On the contrary, some pleasures can be correctly understood only as activities (*energeiai*) and, consequently, as ends. Whereas pleasures leading to the completion of our nature have an end other than themselves, this does not apply to all pleasures (7.12.1153a11–12). Aristotle flatly denies the necessity of believing that there is anything better than pleasure (7.12.1153a7–8). In this argument, he brings together two assertions that suggest a perspective quite foreign to the moral-political horizon that dominates the *Ethics* as a whole: (1) It is not necessary that some other thing be better than pleasure, and (2) some pleasures are desirable for their own sake, that is, not merely because of their formative influence on character.

Aristotle concludes this part of his argument with a definition of pleasure. He disputes the view that pleasure is a "perceived process," defining it instead as the "unimpeded activity of our natural state" (7.12.1153a14–15). Some light is cast on this laconic definition by bringing the immediately preceding argument to bear upon it. Aristotle has just distinguished two categories of pleasures: those leading to the perfection of a natural state and those that are activities of that state once it is fully developed. To recall our earlier examples, the process of eating is pleasurable only to the point of satiety, at which moment it ceases to be pleasant and may even become painful. This is an example of an accidental pleasure, one that is born of deficiency (hunger) and restores us to a normal or healthy condition. On the other hand, Aristotle's example of a pleasure that is not born of deficiency, and consequently does not share this same limitation, is the activity of contemplation. Contemplation is unimpeded activity in the fullest sense because it does not contain within itself the same kind of limit or "impediment" as do bodily pleasures such as eating and drinking.

It is also true that the practice of moral virtue is not subject to the same kind of internal limitations as corporeal activities. One might maintain, as do Gauthier and Jolif, that the definition of pleasure describes the way of life of the *kalos k'agathos* as well as that of the philosopher.[24] This application of Aristotle's definition, however, needs to be qualified in two important respects. First, the economic well-being and social-political status presupposed for the practice of moral virtue constitutes an impediment for those who might lack these advantages. The pleasure of contemplation is less hampered by a lack of external goods than the pleasure of ethical virtue. Second, the *kalos k'agathos* would certainly balk at the suggestion that his life can be described as seeking pleasure, even of a certain kind. In the best case, the *kalos k'agathos* is apt to understand himself in light of the noble. Those "notables" who fall short of the ideal of *kalokagathia* are more likely to view the advantages of good birth, wealth, and education that set them apart from the general population as means to such ends as power, honor, or prestige. Whether Aristotle's audience is inclined to set their sights on the noble, honor, or political power, the suggestion that pleasure, even of a certain kind, is the end for which human beings act continues to reveal a perspective that is in tension with the dominant horizon of the *Ethics*.

Notwithstanding these clarifications, Aristotle's suggestive definition of pleasure as unimpeded activity remains incomplete. It is this fact that has led many scholars to suppose that the account in Book VII is a preliminary draft for Aristotle's more complete treatment of the problem in Book X. Owen raises the major difficulty with this well-worn conjecture. The treatment of pleasure in Book X does not take up the nature of pleasure itself. Whereas Book VII attempts a *definition* of pleasure, even if incomplete and tentative, Book X, as we shall see, prescinds from this question altogether. Despite its more systematic *description* of pleasure, Book X brings us no closer to telling us what it is.

The incompleteness of Aristotle's definition in the present context is consistent with the emphasis on puzzle and discovery that is especially pronounced in Book VII as a whole. In the *Metaphysics*, Aristotle writes: "It is through wonder that men now begin and originally began to philosophize, wondering in the first place at those puzzles most at hand" (*Meta.* 1.2.982b12–14). Even more to the point, the enigmatic conflation of pleasure and activity in Book VII reappears as part of the teaching about the prime mover in the *Metaphysics*. The divine activity of the first principle upon which all of heaven and nature depend is identified with the activity of pleasure (*Meta.* 12.7.1072b16–17). It may be that the completion of Aristotle's unfinished account of pleasure in Book VII is not found in the *Ethics* at all, but is offered to those students who are willing to study Aristotle's explicitly philosophic works—perhaps in large measure because of the way in which he has presented the philosophic life in the political treatises.

## PLEASURE AS THE SUPREME GOOD

Aristotle begins the second and central part of his investigation of pleasure (7.13.1153b7–54a7) with the assertion that "nothing prevents a certain kind of pleasure from being the supreme good (*t'ariston*)." He supports his contention with two brief arguments, each of which brings together pleasure and happiness. If it is true that each state has its unimpeded activity, the activity of all of them or the activity of the one that constitutes happiness would be the most desirable thing there is.[25] But since unimpeded activity is pleasure, happiness must be some form of pleasure (7.13.1153b9–14). The second argument (7.13.1153b14–19) builds on Aristotle's earlier analysis of happiness as "perfect" or "complete" activity (1.7.1097a25–97b21). Since perfect activity is unimpeded, happiness must also be understood in this way. Based on his definition of pleasure as unimpeded activity, Aristotle arrives at the same conclusion; namely, happiness must be pleasure of a certain kind.

It is important that the jarring character of these arguments not escape us.[26] The practical purpose of the *Ethics* as a whole is to help decent individuals orient their lives by a true, rather than illusory, notion of happiness. In Book I, Aristotle had indicated that happiness, as the supreme practical good for human beings, furnishes both the starting point and the end of the study of ethics. Since then, his remarks about happiness have tended to be sparing. The theme reentered his study in an explicit way in the concluding passages of Book VI, where it was associated with neither ethical virtue nor prudence, but with wisdom. Indeed, Aristotle has never explicitly attached happiness to the practice of ethical virtue and, to add insult to injury, he now identifies it, not with noble activities, but with pleasurable ones.[27] Moreover, it is not the sort of pleasure of which all are capable. It would seem, rather, that happiness is the preserve of a small band, those whose lives are given over to the activity of contemplation.

Even if happiness should prove accessible to very few, it is nevertheless sought by everyone. Aristotle turns to this issue in a surprising way in his next argument (7.13.1153b25–54a1). Since all animals, including human ones, seek pleasure, this would seem to indicate that it is the supreme good. Aristotle warns that we should not allow ourselves to be deceived by the fact that all do not pursue the same pleasure, since living beings do not necessarily pursue the pleasures they think and say they do. It is possible that, unbeknownst to them, they actually pursue the same thing, for all things, Aristotle writes, possess something divine by nature (7.13.1153b31–32).

How are we to understand this unexpected train of thought? At the very least, Aristotle's argument invites a kind of self-doubt with respect to those things that one pursues on the ground of their being pleasant. More surprising is the Platonic suggestion about an underlying unity behind the variety of particular pleasures. Most striking is the implication that pleasure, or at least a certain kind of pleasure, is something divine or at least connected to the divine. This suggestion may be intended to reflect a disparity that has become increasingly evident between a universal longing for happiness and the greatly restricted possibility for its fulfillment. Although the desire for happiness provides the starting point and guiding principle for ethics, the harsh truth that Aristotle continues to unveil is that some pleasures, particularly those that constitute the fulfillment of this universal desire, are not within the reach of all.

## PLEASURE AS DIVINE ACTIVITY

The third and final part of the investigation of pleasure in Book VII (7.14.1154a8–54b34) addresses (for the most part) the belief that some pleasures are good, while most are bad. Aristotle begins with a refutation of this view. He then goes on to explain why bodily pleasures seem to be more desirable than others and concludes with a sober teaching on the limited human capacity for pleasure.

Aristotle maintains that bodily pleasures are good in moderation although they are not the sole good (7.14.1154a8–21). The reason why some might think they are bad is that they admit of excess. Persons considered base are not so regarded because they enjoy and pursue bodily pleasures, but rather because they pursue them immoderately or in the wrong way. This problem, however, does not apply to those pleasures that do not admit of excess, because they cannot be in excess of the good (7.14.1154a13–14). Although Aristotle gives no example here, he does make it clear that these cannot be bodily pleasures. Given the arguments of the preceding section, the pleasure of contemplation seems the most likely candidate. This pleasure, which is desirable for its own sake and constitutes happiness insofar as it is accessible to human beings, cannot be in excess of the good.

It is sufficient for our purposes to note that Aristotle offers two related explanations to account for the mistaken belief that bodily pleasures are more desirable than others (7.14.1154a26–b20).[28] First, such pleasures drive out pain. Second, bodily pleasures are sought because of their intensity by those who are incapable of enjoying other pleasures. In the course of this argument, Aristotle alludes to the findings of "natural scientists" (*hoi phusiologoi*) who maintain that a state of strain or toil is the natural condition for living organisms (7.14.1154b7–8). On the basis of their findings, Aristotle explains that most people seek intense bodily pleasures in order to relieve the toil or pain that is part of life itself.

There are, Aristotle observes, two classes of persons apt to seek out intense bodily pleasures (7.14.1154b9–15). The first of these are the young who seek pleasure as a release from the pains involved in growth. The second group, familiar to us from his earlier reference in the first part of Book VII, is comprised of those who possess an ardent or intense nature (*hoi melancholikoi tēn phusin*). In contrast to youth, which is a transient state, the bodies of the *melancholikoi* are in a state of constant irritation in which intense desires and longings are continually active. Aristotle explains that some of those possessing this temperament become profligate or base because they seek out intense restorative pleasures to drive out the pain.

This account is surprising. In a book that aims at fostering ethical virtue, Aristotle has succeeded in offering an explanation as to why someone might become profligate or base that is completely devoid of moral culpability. Profligacy, at least in some cases, results from a natural disposition that keeps the body in a state of constant irritation. This analysis pursues a line of inquiry that is, to say the least, uncharacteristic of the understanding of most decent persons.

Aristotle's argument explains why the *melancholikos* might become profligate while, at the same time, making clear the inadequacy of such a response. What they need is a "perpetual restorative," and, as his earlier arguments have made clear, no amount of *bodily* pleasure can ever supply that want. The proper antidote, insofar as it is available to human beings, must be sought elsewhere. In fact, this will not be a "restorative" at all, but rather pleasure in a strict or unqualified sense. The one needing such pleasure turns out not to be more defective but, potentially at least, healthier than most, for such a person is by nature oriented toward and can be satisfied with nothing less than the activity of those pleasures that do not admit of excess. It would seem that someone so constituted is directed by nature to the kind of unimpeded activity that Aristotle has identified with happiness. If the *melancholikos* is susceptible to profligacy, the argument of *Problems XXX*, as we have seen, maintains that this same disposition also gives rise to different kinds of greatness, including philosophic greatness (see *Pol.* 2.7.1267a2–12).

Aristotle concludes his consideration of pleasure in Book VII with a sober teaching on the limits of human happiness (7.14.1154b20–34). Due to the composite nature of human being, nothing can give us pleasure always; only god enjoys a single, simple pleasure perpetually. Aristotle explains that activity is to be found in both motion and immobility, but that the activity of pleasure is greater in a state of quietude (*hēremia*) than in a state of motion (*kinēsis*) (7.14.1154a26–28). The imperfect unity of a composite nature prevents the continuous enjoyment of this state of quietude by human beings. Aristotle concludes by quoting Euripides: "Change in all things is sweet" but, he adds, owing to some bad thing or deficiency in human beings. Several aspects of this argument warrant further comment.

The concluding description of divine activity provides some explanation for Aristotle's assertion at the outset of Book VII that the categories of virtue and vice are as inappropriate to the gods as they are to the beasts (7.1.1145a25–27). He had introduced the theme of godlike human excellence in this book with a citation from the *Iliad* (7.1. 1145a20–22); he ends Book VII by replacing Homer's poetic myth with philosophic speculation about divine nature (cf. *Meta.* 12. 7.1072b13–31; 12.9.1074b15–45). Aristotle's reflection on the nature and activity of god comes to light, not during his discussion of ethical virtue, but only after putting that discussion aside and starting over again; as such, it furnishes the final and culminating piece for his new beginning.

It could hardly go unnoticed that the activity of god is wholly given over to pleasure. Aristotle's final rumination in Book VII reinforces the arguments of the central section of his account of pleasure; namely, that nothing prevents pleasure from being the supreme good. He describes a god who is removed from the concerns that occupy the lives of most decent persons, a being who is completely self-sufficient and indifferent to things that change, that is, those things that come into being and pass away. There is nothing in this account to suggest that god is concerned about ethical matters or the affairs of humankind; such a deity neither rewards the just nor punishes the wicked. Any attempt to find in divine activity a standard by which to guide one's own life would pose a special problem for the *kaloi k'agathoi*, since they, unlike god, exercise and manifest their virtue precisely in the realm of things that come into being and pass away. The attempt to realize a godlike human excellence, if it does not require that one jettison the standards of moral virtue, appears to render those standards irrelevant or at best secondary. Indeed, the most godlike individual would be wholly given over to the enjoyment of pleasure, albeit of a rare and simple kind.

How then would Aristotle's concluding conjecture affect that group of readers to whom, I have argued, he has been especially attentive throughout Book VII? On the face of it, they would seem to fare better. The only human activity that even approximates divine happiness is the activity of contemplation. If this suggestion is not as disturbing to the potential philosopher as it would be for the nonphilosopher, it nevertheless brings with it a sober and important Aristotelian teaching on the nature and limits of human happiness. Because of our composite nature, even those capable of participating in the most sublime pleasures are not able to do so all the time; other pleasures are both attractive and necessary. Hence, even philosophers must practice continence or ethical virtue with respect to those things that draw them away from the best activity.[29] If philosophers do not take their fundamental bearings from ethical virtue, neither are they able to dismiss those virtues as irrelevant to their own way of life.

More than any other book in the *Ethics*, Book VII departs from the standard of *orthos logos* that provides the dominant horizon for the treatise as a whole. The more extensive use of arguments drawn from dialectic and natural philosophy and, in general, the greater emphasis on puzzle and discovery, reveals that the dominant horizon is not the only or even fundamental one. The radical dissimilarity between the life of the philosopher and that of the *kalos k'agathos* emerges most clearly for those willing to undertake a thoughtful reading of Book VII, rather than minimize its importance on the basis of premature judgments about the ostensibly lower and unfinished character of its arguments. I have been particularly attentive to the provocative implications of Aristotle's new beginning because it is in this way that he invites his most careful readers to contemplate a truth about the unlikeness of the two audiences to whom he has addressed his study.

Needless to say, the *Ethics* does not end at this point. As we shall see, the considerations of friendship, pleasure, and happiness that follow attempt to span the chasm opened by Book VII, bringing to the fore the extent to which the philosophic and ethical ways of life are similar and even complementary. Nevertheless, there remains an essential and ineradicable dissonance between the natural standard of contemplative pleasure and the active life of moral-political excellence, a dissonance that Aristotle will mute but not dispel in the books that follow.

# CHAPTER FOUR

# Virtue, Friendship, and Philosophy, Books VIII–IX

## TURNING TO FRIENDSHIP

Between the two accounts of pleasure in Books VII and X, and in some measure bridging the important differences that separate them, is an unfairly neglected treatment of friendship. Although this part of Aristotle's study is sometimes considered a distinct treatise, its position in the *Ethics* is both important and intelligible. Aristotle's provocative and perhaps disconcerting analysis of pleasure in Book VII is followed by an inquiry that pulls pleasure back into the orbit of moral virtue: Every friendship is based on goodness or pleasure and, in the best case, it is based on both (8.3.1156b19–24). The pleasure that decent persons take in the company of their friends affords an unobjectionable way to reflect on the place and importance of pleasure in human life. The examination of friendship in Books VIII and IX clears the way for a thematic reconsideration of pleasure at the beginning of Book X.

It should be noted at the outset that the Aristotelian and, in general, Greek conception of friendship (*philia*) is broader than that designated by standard English usage. *Philia* does not refer primarily to intimate relationships outside the family, but covers the full range of familial relationships as well (parents to children, children to parents, relations among siblings, and the primary relationship between husband and wife). *Philia* is also used to describe the bonds of citizenship; political friendship is a meaningful category of analysis for Aristotle. Moreover, the word applies to a variety of relationships that stand between the family and the polis, such as the relationship among members of religious and social clubs as well as different types of political or military associations. The common thread binding the broad range of relationships subsumed under the category of *philia* derives from the natural tendency of political animals to develop a sense of concern for the various individuals and groups with whom they are knit together in the warp and woof of human life.

Aristotle asserts that friendship is necessary for human beings and, as such, constitutes an appropriate topic of consideration. Among the several specific reasons for the inquiry that follows, three stand out and in some way encompass the rest: Friendship bears directly on virtue and politics; it also seems to be natural. Each of these initial reasons for studying friendship warrants further comment.

Aristotle begins with the statement that friendship is virtue of a certain kind or is "with" (*meta*) virtue (8.1.1155a3–4). Although the needed explanation is deferred until later, his introductory remarks emphasize the necessity of friendship in any choiceworthy life. Both the successful and the unsuccessful need friends as do the young, old, and those in their prime. If friendship is a virtue or somehow involves virtue and is indispensable for a choiceworthy human life, then it is an essential topic of investigation in an inquiry that attempts to clarify the nature of human flourishing.

A second reason for turning to an examination of friendship is its relationship to politics (8.1.1155a22–28). Friendship appears to hold the city together (*sunechein*). Consequently, a consideration of friendship is especially useful for legislators since they must concern themselves with "concord" (*homonoia*) or, as it is later called, "political friendship." Aristotle asserts that legislators are even more serious about civic friendship than they are about justice (8.1.1155a22–24). It is not that they are or should be unconcerned about justice, but that friendship or at least political friendship in some way incorporates those concerns. Whereas friends do not need justice, just people still need friends. Justice at its best seems to be a part of friendship (8.1.1155a26–28; cf. *EE* 7.10.1243a10–14).

Aristotle ties together and expands these initial reasons for studying friendship with the assertion that friendship is not only necessary but noble (8.1.1155a28–31). His reference to the noble reinserts a standard that, although never entirely absent, has lost the prominent position it occupied in the discussion of ethical virtue. The appeal to the noble both recalls earlier portions of the *Ethics* and anticipates later discussions in the *Politics*, where Aristotle explains that legislators aim at providing for both the requirements of living and living well. In the present context, he indicates that friendship somehow bears on both dimensions of life in the city and, as such, is or should be of crucial importance to legislators. It is important to note that these initial statements about friendship are provisional. By connecting friendship to the themes of virtue and politics, Aristotle provides his readers with two good reasons for including the topic in his treatise, although he has not as yet clarified his own teaching on these points.

In addition, Aristotle briefly inserts a third reason for this inquiry (8.1.1155a16–22). Friendship appears to be natural (*phusei*). Members of the same species, and most especially the human species, have a natural friendship with each other, something that is discernible even among strangers thrown together by travel. The fact that the phenomenon of friendship, especially as it pertains to the relationship between parents and offspring, repeats itself in different and foreign cultures and even in different animal species, is put forward as an indication of its naturalness.

These three reasons for turning to the study of friendship provide two distinct frames or standards for the inquiry that follows. Friendship is necessary to human life both because it is something natural and because of its importance for civic life. The case of moral virtue falls in between. As we have already seen, the capacity for moral virtue comes from nature, although its realization occurs as a result of habits developed in relationship with others, that is, through the training and opportunities provided by the various associations found in the city (2.1.1103a14–03b25). It is important to observe how Aristotle shifts from one standard to the other. As we shall see, a full appreciation for the place and importance of friendship in the *Ethics* is, at its highest, generated by the tension between the desire to live one's life in accord with nature and the necessity of doing so within the confines of the city.


FRIENDSHIP AND VIRTUE


A discussion of the nature and kinds of friendship clarifies the meaning of Aristotle's initial assertion that friendship is a virtue or "with" virtue. The consideration begins with the observation that the lovable (*to philēton*) falls into one of three categories: the good, the pleasant, or the useful (8.2.1155b17–19). This, in turn, leads to three kinds of friendship: friendship based on utility, pleasure friendship, and "perfect" or "complete" (*teleios*) friendship.[1] This last kind of friendship exists

among the good who resemble each other in virtue. In this case, friends
are loved for their own sake since, unlike utility or pleasure friendships,
friends are loved for who they are and not because of some accidental
or temporary quality (*kata sumbebēkos*). Whereas the particular pleasure or usefulness that gives rise to friendship based on pleasure or utility is often temporary, the virtue that anchors perfect friendship is
steadfast (*monimos*) because it is rooted in character. Moreover,
friendship among the good in some way incorporates the other two
kinds of friendship, since the good are also useful and pleasurable to
each other. Aristotle concludes that it is among the virtuous that friendship exists in its fullest (*malista*) and best (*aristē*) form (8.3.1156b22–
24). This is friendship in its primary or proper sense and I will refer to
it in this way in the treatment that follows. In light of these explanations,
it would seem that friendships based on utility or pleasure do not,
strictly speaking, qualify as friendship except in an analogous sense
(8.4.1157a30–32).[2]

This initial definition and classification of friendship builds upon
and is consistent with Aristotle's teaching on ethical virtue, although
the exact relationship between them is not yet fully clarified. If it is true
that primary friendship presupposes moral virtue, it is not clear
whether moral virtue, by itself, insures friendship. To state the question
with greater precision, if moral virtue is a necessary condition for
friendship, is it a sufficient one?

The answer emerges clearly from Aristotle's subsequent specification of the several additional attributes of friendship implicit in his initial definition. He explains that it is necessary for friends to be aware of
the goodwill that each has for the other. In the best case, this means that
friends must know of one another's virtue. Such knowledge results
from trying and testing (*dokimazō*) one's friend over a long period of
time (8.4.1157a21–22). Coming to know and trust in the reality of
another's virtue presupposes a variety of shared experiences so that an
individual's good character can become visible to a friend.

A second characteristic of friends is that they want to be in each
other's company. Whereas two virtuous people retain their virtue when
separated, and are thereby likely to retain some degree of friendship as
well, prolonged absence causes the friendship to diminish (8.5.1157b11–
12). Hence, Aristotle insists that nothing is more characteristic of friends
than the desire to live together (*suzēn*) (8.5.1157b19).

This aspect of friendship delicately points to a third, namely, the key
importance of pleasure. Human beings do not wish to pass their days

in the company of those whose presence fails to please since it is only natural to avoid what is painful and seek what is pleasant (8.5.1157b13–17). Indeed, it is impossible for friends to spend time together unless they give one another pleasure or in some way delight each other (8.5.1157b22–23). The natural desire for pleasure plays a central role not only in pleasure friendships, but also in those that are grounded in moral goodness. This is because, as Aristotle repeatedly observes, the morally serious person furnishes the appropriate human standard for both goodness and pleasure. In the present context, he explains that good human beings love that which is good and pleasurable simply as well as that which is good and pleasurable for themselves (8.5.1157b25–28). Pleasure or utility friendships are based only on the latter condition. Aristotle's emphasis on the role of pleasure and delight in friendship applies most directly to primary friendship. In this case, the pleasure is not accidental but intrinsic to the relationship, since it arises from a true perception of the good character of one's friend (cf. *EE* 7.2.1237a40–37b6).

Aristotle next takes up the case of those for whom age or perhaps illness has eroded their good temper and capacity to enjoy the company of others. Such persons may still be characterized by goodwill toward one another and, as evidence of their abiding virtue, are willing to help each other whenever there is need. Yet, they cannot properly be called friends because they no longer seek or enjoy each other's company (8.6.1158a1–10). This case reveals the way in which fortune affects friendship. The effects of aging or long disease may not destroy one's good character, but they do diminish friendship.[3] The bearing of fortune on the possibility of friendship parallels its influence on happiness. In Book I, Aristotle had gone to great lengths to argue that virtue and not fortune is the cause of happiness for a human being, although he also acknowledged that grave misfortune necessarily mars supreme happiness (1.10.1101a6–8). Similarly, he now argues that virtue provides the core condition for friendship. However, the case of the elderly suggests that such friendships are not unaffected by adverse conditions not entirely or not at all within human control.

A fifth characteristic of friendship in some way results from those that have preceded it. Aristotle explains that friendship proper is something rare. He offers several reasons, some of which recapitulate what has gone before. Not only are the number of good persons always likely to be in a minority, but there is also a need to test the friendship as well as a need to live together in a way that allows for intimacy (*sunētheia*).

Both require time and are difficult to do (8.6.1158a14–15). There is, however, an additional reason for its infrequency. Just as erotic love tends toward exclusivity by nature (*phusei*); it is not easy to please with any intensity (*areskein sphodra*) many people at the same time (8.6.1158a13–14). If there are several reasons why friendship in the full sense is rare, one at least is grounded in a natural inability to sustain friendship with many people simultaneously. Although it is not problematic to have several acquaintances with people who are characterized by moral goodness, the same cannot be said of genuine friendship.

In bringing to light the various characteristics implicit in his initial classification, Aristotle makes it clear that virtue is a necessary but not a sufficient condition for friendship. Although the argument does not imply that there is any tension between moral virtue and friendship, it gently introduces the idea that friendship is rarer and, in some sense at least, more complete or perfect than moral virtue. Since the absence of friendship seriously impoverishes human happiness even among the virtuous, friendship may prove more desirable than moral virtue insofar as it contributes to happiness in a way that virtue by itself does not.

## FRIENDSHIP AND THE CITY

Readers are gradually moved toward a second reason for considering friendship—namely, its relationship to the city—by means of a comparison between justice and friendship. This comparison is especially apt for two reasons. As we have seen, Aristotle's initial account of comprehensive justice encompassed the whole of virtue toward others (5.1.1130a3–13). Comprehensive justice is akin to friendship and, as the social or political virtue par excellence, it is also directly tied to the political community. Indeed, as Aristotle explains in the *Politics*, justice is the ordering or organizing principle for the polis (*Pol.* 1.3.1253a37–39). The second reason for this comparison derives from Aristotle's earlier consideration of political justice. That account revealed the limits of justice as it is actually found in existing cities, and pointed to the need for a higher standard exhibited in the actions, disposition, and wisdom of the equitable person. In the measure that political justice is reduced to a quasi-mathematical canon of mutual obligations, the treatment of friendship, particularly political friendship, provides a necessary supplement by taking into account a more generous human capacity for mutual concern that deepens and humanizes the various ties that bind citizens together in a political partnership.

The most obvious kinship between justice and friendship stems from the fact that both look toward others. Aristotle explains and contrasts this kinship with reference to equality. Both justice and friendship involve equality although the precise nature of the equality is different in each case (8.7.1158b29–33). Justice is primarily proportional equality (*kat'axian*) and, secondarily, equality according to quantity or extent (*kata poson*), whereas friendship reverses these priorities.[4] Hence a wide gulf in virtue, wealth, political power, goodness, or wisdom precludes friendship (8.7.1158b33–59a3) but not justice, since proportional equality accommodates a greater degree of dissimilarity. Although there is no fixed point at which inequality destroys friendship, a limit case is provided by the gods. If one were to become so greatly superior to another that the proportion were comparable to that which separates a god from a human being, friendship would no longer be possible (8.7.1159a3–5), although Aristotle implies that the demands of justice would still hold.[5]

In the course of this argument, Aristotle introduces a puzzle that is not fully addressed until Book IX. Is it true, he asks, that we wish our friends the greatest goods for their own sake (8.7.1159a5–12)? For instance, would we want them to become gods or at least godlike? In that case the disparity would become so great that we would lose them as friends. Aristotle offers a partial solution by saying that we wish our friends the greatest goods consistent with their remaining human. Although this appears to settle the limit case, it does not entirely resolve the problem. Even if the discrepancy were not so great as that between divine and human beings, Aristotle has just indicated that lesser inequalities in virtue, wealth, power, goodness, and wisdom are sufficient to destroy friendship. The question remains: Is it possible to wish even the greatest goods compatible with being human for one's friends if that means losing them as friends? In the present context, Aristotle restricts himself to a tentative suggestion that anticipates the important theme of self-love to which he will return in Book IX. Perhaps one does not wish a friend all of these goods, for human beings wish good things for themselves most of all (8.7.1159a11–12).

The initial contrast between friendship and justice is followed by an examination of the degree to which friendship and justice are coextensive. In every association there seems to be some sort of justice as well as friendship. Sailors, soldiers, members of religious guilds, and dining companions all share a kind of friendship that is proportionate to the distinctive good aimed at by their particular partnership. All such partnerships are embraced by the larger association of the polis, which aims not at partial or temporary advantages but at all the goods necessary for life (8.9.1160a21–23). Insofar as the less comprehensive partnerships form parts of a larger whole, each of these friendships is subordinate to the more inclusive association provided by the city itself (8.9.1160a28–30).

Aristotle proceeds to describe the variety of regimes and, in each case, a corresponding type of friendship. The three decent regimes are kingship, aristocracy, and one based on property qualification that is best described as "timocracy" although it is most often referred to as polity. Aristotle simply asserts that kingship is the best of the decent regimes and timocracy the worst. Among the deviant or perverse regimes, tyranny is the worst, whereas democracy is the least bad and only a slight departure from the decent regime of polity or timocracy. In each case, similar patterns of friendship can be found in the less inclusive partnerships of which the polis is comprised. This is most apparent in the household. The relationship between father and son resembles kingship but becomes more like tyranny if children are reduced to the status of slaves. The friendship between husband and wife mirrors aristocracy insofar as it is based on the relative virtue of each and assigns to each what is fitting. This degenerates into something like oligarchy if the husband controls everything without regard to the proper worth of his spouse. Friendship among brothers corresponds to timocracy, where equal and decent citizens rule in turn and on equal terms. This becomes more like democracy when equality supersedes every concern for merit or worth. Aristotle concludes that friendship appears in each regime to the extent that justice does (8.11.1161a10–11). In the deviant regimes, justice is found only to a slight degree, something that is also true of friendship (8.11.1161a30–32).

Several points follow from this classification of regimes and the kinds of friendship that most reflect them. Although Aristotle does not explain why kingship is best, he indicates elsewhere that justice would seem to require this arrangement in political communities containing individuals of extraordinary virtue (*Pol.* 3.13.1284b25–34; 3.17.1288a15–29). The elevation of kingship in the present context is consistent with his earlier description of justice as proportional equality. That same discussion, however, reminds us that among decent regimes kingship is least congenial to the full flowering of friendship since friendship is based on simple equality. Indeed, the possibility of friendship is greatest in a timocracy where decent citizens rule in turns and by equal shares (8.11.1161a25–30). If timocracy is the worst of the decent regimes from the point of view of justice, it is the best regime from the point of view of friendship. The two goods of political wisdom and broad civic participation are not easily reconciled. This tension does not, however, invalidate the dominant argument of these chapters since there is, in most cases, a significant overlap between justice and friendship. Nevertheless, the symmetry between them is not as perfect as we might have initially thought. Indeed, in the best case, a serious concern for either justice or friendship could lead legislators to adopt different kinds of regimes.

Aristotle's parallel account of particular kinds of regimes and the different sorts of friendship that arise within them is indicative of the fact that any given regime subtly colors a citizen's understanding of friendship. The deeper issue is that friendship, as it is typically experienced, is not simply natural; it is always mediated by the regime in which one lives. Fully natural friendship would require one to transcend the pervasive civic optic laid down by the regime or, to draw upon Plato's image, it would require that one leave the cave. However, it is important to observe that even while Aristotle explains the priority of the political partnership over the partial associations it engenders, he never entirely views friendship from within this horizon. The clearest evidence for this lies in the fact that he never draws the relevant conclusion regarding friendship. Although the polis is the most authoritative association, nowhere does he assert that civic or political friendship is the most authoritative form of friendship. Instead, Aristotle suggests the existence of a tension or lack of symmetry between the requirements of justice and those of friendship.

How then are we to understand Aristotle's apparently conflicting assessments of the relative priority of friendship and justice? In the order of necessity, the polis, which is bound together by some understanding of justice, is properly regarded as prior. It is the most authoritative partnership because it includes and makes possible every other association, including friendship. As a part of this larger whole, friendship is necessarily shaped, though not always consciously, by the type of regime in which it is found. Friendship is, in this sense, subordinate to the city and the particular understanding of justice by which the city is ordered. However, we have also noted Aristotle's earlier suggestion that friendship is a better thing than justice (8.1.1155a22–28; cf. *EE*

7.10.1243a10–14). Without in any way withdrawing the priority that he assigns to the city in the order of necessity or its authority as the most comprehensive association, the discussion of friendship points to a kind of excellence that, although less comprehensive and less authoritative, is nevertheless more desirable than either justice or citizenship. The higher status of friendship and its bearing on the city will become increasingly evident as the analysis unfolds. A first step in this direction is taken in the final chapters of Book VIII when Aristotle turns to the greater claims that can be made on behalf of friendship in the order of nature.

## FRIENDSHIP AND NATURE

Book VIII concludes with practical advice about a number of problems regarding friendship. Most pertinent for our purposes is the distinction between friendships that exist among kin and companions, and those that arise because of a certain agreement or compact (*kath'homologian tina*), such as friendship among citizens, tribesmen, shipmates, and the like (8.12.1161b11–15). Aristotle divides friendship into those kinds that arise naturally and those that arise through convention.[6] He then goes on to discuss the various sorts of kinship falling within the first category despite the fact that he has just discussed them from the point of view of the city, that is, on the basis of their similarity to the different types of regimes.

Unlike his preceding analysis, Aristotle's reconsideration of household friendships treats them on their own terms. All such friendships derive from the parental relationship (8.12.1161b16–62a16). Parents love their children as other selves because they are part of themselves and yet exist as separate beings. Children love their parents as the source of their being and insofar as they come from them by nature (*ap'ekeinōn pephukota*). Siblings likewise love each other because they are by nature out of the same parents (*ek tōn autōn pephukenai*). Consequently, they are in some way the same, a shared identity that is strengthened by a common upbringing and similarity in age. Friendship between husband and wife also appears to be natural (*kata phusin*) since human beings are by nature pairing creatures more than political ones, inasmuch as the household is prior to and more necessary than the city and the activity of procreation is characteristic of animals in general (8.12.1162a16–19).[7] Aristotle's reconsideration of friendship within the family focuses on the natural source of these relationships as they spring from the act of generation, something that is not dependent upon a particular kind of regime nor restricted to a single species.

If all forms of friendship exist within the more inclusive partnership provided by the polis and are thereby necessarily affected by the particular character of that association, the claim that friendship, in some sense, transcends the regime stems from the fact that it is more natural. From the point of view of the regime, the household is a subordinate community, but from the standpoint of nature it must be given precedence. Aristotle had originally proposed the topic of friendship because of its relationship to moral virtue and politics; he now suggests that it is more natural than either moral virtue or the polis. Aristotle's analysis invites readers to reflect on a dimension of their experience that exists within the city but is most immediately rooted in nature.

The two most important pieces of unfinished business at the close of Book VIII are the unanswered question about the status of self-love and the promised treatment of political friendship. Both of these topics are taken up in Book IX. To these issues, it is necessary to add a third: the place and importance of the theoretical life. The consideration that follows focuses especially on these three themes as well as the way in which the discussion in Book IX prepares readers for a final and explicit ranking of ethical and theoretical excellence in Book X.[8]


## FRIENDSHIP WITH ONESELF

As we have noted, the problem of self-love made its first appearance as part of a response to an unresolved puzzle, namely, whether it is possible to wish the greatest goods for our friends, given a pervasive human tendency to wish good things most of all for oneself (8.7.1159a5–12). We are brought one step closer to a thematic consideration of self-love by means of a second aporetic reflection, this time dealing with the very possibility of friendship with oneself. Aristotle tentatively suggests that friendship with others seems to derive from a prior friendship that decent persons have with themselves (9.4.1166a1–2). The evidence for this suggestion is furnished by means of a contrast between the interior states of morally serious and morally base (*phauloi*) persons.

Decent persons are of one mind and desire the same things with every part of their soul. They wish for their own good for their own sake and seek it through action. They also desire their own life and preservation. This pertains especially to the rational part of the soul since it would appear that the thinking part is what each one is, or at least it is more the self than anything else (9.4.1166a22–23).[9] The good desire their own company since they have agreeable memories of the past and good hopes for the future. Their mind is, as Aristotle puts is, well stored with subjects for contemplation. Finally, the decent are keenly aware of their own joys and sorrows since, owing to their good character, the same things give rise to either pleasure or pain (rather than different things at different times).

Aristotle simply observes that these same attitudes characterize friendship, an observation that leads to his famous characterization of a friend as "another self" (*allos autos*) (9.4.1166a29–33).[10] Although he never says whether the notion of friendship with oneself is, strictly speaking, meaningful, he does maintain that it possesses a certain plausibility given the dual or composite nature of human being (9.4.1166a34–66b1). The same argument had been entertained but rejected with respect to justice. Aristotle had ruled out the possibility of justice with oneself, except in an attenuated and metaphorical sense, because of the essential relationship between justice and the polis (5.11.1138b5–13). His more open-ended argument in the present context is consistent with the fact that friendship enjoys a status that is somehow distinct from the public or common good of the city.

The depiction of the interior state of the decent is contrasted with a corresponding description of the morally base. The latter are characterized by one or more of the following deficiencies. Unlike the decent, they lack unity of soul because they are constantly at odds with themselves. They desire one thing and yet choose another. Although they might wish for their own good, they fail to do what is necessary to attain it out of cowardice or idleness. Life is not desirable for the morally base and in the most extreme cases they seek to end it. They are unable to be by themselves because they recall or anticipate much that is unpleasant. They are also unable to enter into their own joys and sorrows because there is factional conflict (*stasiazō*) in their souls. The same things can give rise to both joy and sorrow and these are in a constant state of flux. The bad are devoid of affection for themselves for the simple reason that there is nothing truly lovable about them.

This morally edifying contrast between the decent and the base concludes with a rare moral exhortation: Given the misery to which the base are subject, readers should do their utmost to flee wickedness and seek decency (9.4.1166b26–29). Heeding such counsel leads to friend-ship both with oneself and with others. By clarifying the interior states of the decent and the wicked, Aristotle has made apparent how much more desirable the former condition is than the latter. At the same time, however, he uses this morally edifying distinction to advance a more controversial claim. As he begins to lay bare the psychological root for friendship, Aristotle points to the primary importance of self-love.[11]

## POLITICAL FRIENDSHIP

Before turning in a direct way to the problem of self-love, Aristotle undertakes a consideration of three qualities that are similar to, but not the same as, friendship (goodwill, concord, and beneficence). It is within this context that he offers his fullest evaluation of political friendship, a discussion that has been awaited since the outset of Book VIII. It is surprisingly brief.

Political or civic friendship (*politikē philia*) is identified with "con-cord" or, more literally, "oneness of mind" (*homonoia*) (9.6.1167b2–3). The first part of Aristotle's account is a description of concord as it exists within a polis (9.6.1167a22–67b4). Concord does not result from unanimity about any subject whatever, but is the particular sort of agreement characteristic of citizens about practical matters of direct civic importance. For example, concord exists among citizens when they are of one mind concerning the basic structure of the regime, a par-ticular foreign alliance, or the selection of a ruler. More generally, the polis is characterized by *homonoia* when citizens agree about what is advantageous, adopt the same policy, and carry their common resolves into action. This like-mindedness among citizens is typically identified with political friendship.

The second part of Aristotle's clarification is based on a contrast between the decent and the base (9.6.1167b4–16). *Homonoia* is char-acteristic of decent persons since they are of one mind both with them-selves and with one another. As a result, their wishes are more or less constant, especially with respect to the effort to secure in common that which is just and advantageous for the city. The base, on the other hand, are only capable of concord to a small degree, if at all, since they are characterized by the desire to get for themselves more of the advantages and fewer of the burdens of political life. Far from being of one mind with their fellow citizens, they scrutinize and watch over them, trying to compel others to do the very things that they attempt to avoid for themselves. The result of this mutual suspicion is discord (*stasis*), in which the common interests of the political community are destroyed by a narrow and mistrustful preoccupation with self-interest.

Although there can be no concord among the base by themselves, Aristotle does allow that political friendship sometimes extends to the many (*dēmos*). This is possible when they agree with the decent that the best should rule (9.6.1167a34–67b1). A fuller explanation of this compressed statement is provided in the *Politics*. Whereas the many who make up a multitude lack individual excellence, they can become better if joined together into a single whole. The absence of complete virtue in any particular member is ameliorated in a collective body in the measure that the discrete parts of virtue embodied in each individual contributes to comprehensive excellence on the part of the whole (*Pol.* 3.11.1281a42–81b15). This can only happen, however, if the multitude shares political authority with a virtuous minority. Aristotle explains that the many taken together possess qualities sufficient for deliberating and judging, but that important offices should be reserved for those who most embody political virtue. The result of this "mixing" is beneficial to the city, "just as impure substance mixed with pure makes the whole more useful" (*Pol.* 3.11.1281b22–38). The mixing in question is based on a fundamental agreement among heterogenous citizens that the best should rule. The "more useful" substance produced by this mixture is *homonoia* within the civic association as a whole, something that insures the domestic stability of a regime.

For all the brevity of his discussion in the *Nicomachean Ethics*, Aristotle has succeeded in evaluating political friendship from two distinct vantage points: that provided by the city and that furnished by the decent. In the former case, concord among citizens is the result of practical agreement about what is advantageous; in the latter, it describes a psychic state characteristic of decent persons that enables them to pursue just and advantageous things in common. As we shall see, the shift from a civic to a psychic frame of reference anticipates the discussion of self-love that is soon to follow. Of more immediate importance, this shift raises a question about the nature of political friendship itself: Is it a form of utility friendship based on the mutually advantageous practices of citizens or is it some variation of virtue friendship as it is practiced among the good? The brevity and ambiguity of Aristotle's account in the *Nicomachean Ethics* requires further clarification.

In the *Eudemian Ethics*, we encounter the unambiguous claim that political friendship is based on utility; citizens no longer remember one another once they cease to be useful to each other (*EE* 7.10.1242a7–9; 1242b22–27). Indeed, Aristotle asserts that justice resides especially in utility friendship since utility constitutes political justice (*EE* 7.10.1242a12–14). This would seem to shed light on Aristotle's claim that the political nature of human beings is indicated by their inclination to form partnerships based on a shared perception of the advantageous and the just (*Pol.* 1.2.1253a14–18). If this were all that Aristotle said on the subject, the ambiguity of his statements in the *Nicomachean Ethics* would be dispelled: Political friendship would appear to be a species of utility friendship, and the content of Aristotle's well-known and axiomatic identification of political justice with the common good would mean nothing more than a common or shared perception of the useful.[12]

Aristotle, however, continues with a distinction between legal and ethical species of utility friendship (*EE* 7.10.1242b32–43b39). Whereas legal or political friendship presupposes an explicit agreement to return compensation, the ethical version of utility friendship is based on trust. It is especially the ethical type that is subject to recriminations since implicit agreements based in trust are more liable to misunderstanding than those that have been made explicit by some kind of contract. Frequent dissension also distinguishes the ethical form of utility friendship from friendship among the virtuous, since the emphasis on getting what one deserves or at least what one believes oneself to deserve is foreign to the preoccupation with virtue characteristic of friendship in its primary and best sense. The problem lies in the fact that trust is only *fully* appropriate among decent persons, whereas the ethical version of utility friendship is motivated by an uneven and volatile mix of utility and trust. Aristotle explains that friendship among good persons does not take its bearings from the useful and necessary obligations imposed by law (*dikē*) since they do not approach each other as signatories under contract, but as good and trustworthy human beings on account of the decency of their characters (*EE* 7.10.1243a10–14). Indeed, the primary and natural meaning of *homonoia* is said to be agreement among morally serious persons on matters pertaining to the common life (*EE* 7.7.1241a16–28).

Aristotle's distinction between legal and ethical forms of utility friendship culminates with the contrast between virtue friendship among the decent on the one hand, and the legal and ethical varieties of utility friendship on the other. The contrast between friendship in its primary and best sense and political friendship is not, however, as clear cut as one might initially suppose. The complication arises from Aristotle's teaching on the nature of the civic association itself. Whereas it is true that the political partnership comes into being to satisfy the requirements of living (i.e., the shared advantage of its members), it exists for the sake of living well (*Pol.* 1.2.1252b29–30; 3.9.1280b29–35). Aristotle repeatedly insists that living well cannot be reduced to useful exchange or mutual security, but embraces the loftier aim of noble action (*Pol.* 3.9.1280a31–81a4). Political friendship inevitably slides into ethical friendship; indeed, it aspires to be ethical friendship in its primary sense, the kind of friendship that encourages virtuous action among citizens.[13]

We are now in a position to return to Aristotle's account of political friendship in the *Nicomachean Ethics*. Whereas civic friendship is generally grounded in the low but solid concern of citizens with utility, the desire and need to promote virtuous living among citizens means that political friendship contains an inescapable ethical dimension as well. Aristotle's shift from the vantage point of utility to that provided by virtue reflects an irreducible heterogeneity in the purpose of the civic association itself. It is now possible to understand the way in which the account of political friendship bears on Aristotle's earlier account of justice. As we have seen, an initial, exalted view of comprehensive justice as virtue toward others was gradually displaced by a realistic treatment of the principles of political justice. Political friendship arises from the natural desire of citizens to share something more than the economic and security issues that furnish the necessary, if rudimentary, content for political justice. The something more in question is a citizen's capacity for human excellence. This latter aim is only fully attained among decent human beings who reveal the content of civic like-mindedness at its highest. Although the political partnership can never succeed in becoming a community of friends in this sense, a judicious mixing of the few who are virtuous with the many who are not points to a kind of unanimity that is both more accessible and always in need of encouragement. Aristotle never resolves the tension between the lower and pervasive preoccupation with public utility and the human capacity for noble deeds.[14] It is, rather, the hallmark of prudent statesmen to work within the confines of a given regime to maximize the degree of solidarity or concord possible for a particular civic body. Fostering concord among citizens, at whatever level they are capable of sustaining it, is a matter of urgent concern for legislators since its absence produces the kind of factional conflict (*stasiazō*) that can destroy a city (*Pol.* 2.4.1262b7–10; cf. 5.1.1301a19–02a15).

If the political utility of concord is plain for all to see, the same cannot be said of its status as a kind of friendship. Concord would seem to qualify as friendship only in an analogous sense. Even though the primary and natural meaning of concord is found among morally decent citizens, moral virtue is, as we have seen, a necessary but insufficient condition for friendship. It would be impossible for all such citizens to know one another, much less test each other over a long period of time. It is certainly impossible for them to live together except in the attenuated sense of living in the same city. Moreover, if it is only possible to have a few friends and friendship is something rare, this could not apply to a body of citizens whose relations with each other are numerous and common. In light of these earlier clarifications, it is clear that political friendship falls short of friendship proper. What then is the exact relationship between concord and friendship, and how is Aristotle using that relationship in the *Ethics*?

The clearest answer to this question is that friendship supplies a standard that can be applied in a watered down way to the civic body as a whole.[15] Aristotle draws upon the experience of friendship among the good to suggest the inadequacy of a political compact limited to or determined by the principles of distributive, commutative, and reciprocal justice. The existence of a certain kind of friendship among citizens is more desirable in that it provides a better and appropriate cohesiveness for the polis as a whole. Concord turns an aggregate of individuals, seeking their own advantage and suspiciously watching the actions of others, into a single community. If, as Aristotle says, political friendship only actually exists among the decent (or, in the broadest case, depends upon them), legislators should be concerned to carry out policies that foster moral seriousness among citizens. Promoting this end presupposes a concern for moral education as well as an awareness on the part of legislators of the formative influence of the regime in shaping the souls of citizens.

The experience of friendship among the good turns out to have a limited, although important, analogue in the city. The cultivation of political friendship is, or should be, a central aim of the legislator's art. It does not, however, exhaust the reality of friendship. Aristotle's rich and complex examination of this subject clearly indicates that the most authoritative standard for friendship is not drawn from the public bonds that unite citizens and secure the stability of the city, but from private relationships among the good. His treatise on friendship effectively brings to light a private activity that, while presupposing the authoritative association of the city and contributing to its well-being, transcends it in rank and dignity.

It is from the perspective of private friendships among citizens that Aristotle now addresses a puzzle regarding unequal friendships: Why is it that the benefactor loves the beneficiary more than the beneficiary loves the benefactor (9.7.1167b17–68a27)? The most widespread explanation is drawn from politics and, more specifically, from the principles of economic exchange that dominate civic life. The benefactor, like a creditor, has a vested interest in the safety of the beneficiary whereas the beneficiary, like the debtor, would gladly have the benefactor out of the way. Although Aristotle thinks that this harsh analogy captures something true about human beings, it fails to explain the kind of friendship that arises in this situation. The limits of this account become apparent in light of a more natural (*phusikōteron*) explanation (9.7.1167b28–68a9). The benefactor is more like a craftsman than a creditor. In the same way that poets love their poems and parents love their children, benefactors also love their handiwork. The reason for this is that human beings love most what they have brought into existence.[16] Moreover, the love for what we have brought into being is ultimately based on a more primary love for one's own being that expresses itself in activity (9.7.1168a5–6). It is a general principle of nature that the potential (*dunamis*) of a thing is made actual through its proper work or activity (9.7.1168a8–9). For doers of beneficent deeds, the activity that best expresses their potential is a beneficent act. Benefactors are naturally inclined to love their deed and everything pertaining to it because their activity and its memory actualize the primary love that they have for their own existence. For beneficiaries, on the other hand, the same act evokes an awareness of some incompleteness in their life. However grateful for the help they have received, beneficiaries are less capable of loving their own existence precisely because of the deficiency that occasioned the beneficent deed in the first place.

Aristotle's explanation reveals more about human nature than the pervasive but narrowly political one. His turn to the insights of natural philosophy is, at the same time, a return to the thorny question of self-love. It is not reciprocal justice among citizens but a primary and natural love that human beings feel for their own existence that best elucidates a phenomenon which, though it approaches friendship, falls short of its fullest expression.[17]

## TWO KINDS OF SELF-LOVE

Aristotle is now ready to address head on the question whether one ought to love oneself or someone else most (9.8.1168a28–69b2). He begins by sketching two sides of a debate. On one side, self-love is usually taken to be a term of opprobrium. Whereas the base do everything for their own sake, the decent are willing to act for the sake of their friends while putting their own concerns aside. Hence, love for others would seem to take priority over self-love. On the other side of the question, as Aristotle has already argued (9.4.1166a1–66b29), all feelings of friendship toward others seem to be an extension of self-love since the conditions for friendship also describe a more primary relationship that persons have with themselves. Insofar as an individual is his or her own best friend, the argument suggests that one ought to love oneself most.

Aristotle acknowledges that each of these positions makes some sense and proposes to unravel the resulting puzzle by considering more carefully the precise meaning that each side attaches to self-love (*philautos*). The kind of self-love that is rightly blamed is the kind that is most in evidence. Those who love most the lower part of their soul assign a larger portion of money, honor, or bodily pleasure to themselves. Self-love in this sense leads many people to indulge their appetites and passions, that is, the irrational part of the soul. It is precisely because this is the most pervasive meaning of self-love that the term is generally and correctly used as a term of censure. However, this is not the truest meaning of self-love. The person who is always striving to secure the noble, practices each of the virtues in an exemplary way. Such persons are hardly blameworthy and yet they would seem to be self-lovers to an exceptional degree. The reason for this is that they take their bearings from the best and most authoritative part of themselves, namely intelligence (*nous*). By loving and gratifying the part of their soul that is, or is most, their true self, such persons prove to be lovers of self in the truest sense. Aristotle concludes that the good ought to be lovers of self and that by doing noble deeds they benefit both themselves and others (9.8.1169a11–13).

The concluding part of the argument in this chapter spells out the consequences for friends and country of self-love properly understood

(9.8.1169a18–34). Those who seek to gain the noble for themselves are willing to part with money, honors, and offices to advance the good of friends and fatherland. They may even be willing to make the supreme sacrifice of their lives if circumstances warrant it. In each case, however, the individuals in question are choosing the better part because they choose to make the noble their own through action. In taking a larger share of the noble for themselves, that is, in loving themselves most of all, morally serious persons also benefit friends and fellow citizens, sometimes in extraordinary ways.

This argument emphasizes the extent to which self-love is compatible with friendship and patriotism without drawing attention to the limits of that compatibility. Aristotle is able to reveal a broad and deep conflux between self-love, friendship, and the city by appealing to the noble, the lofty standard to which he has often directed his readers throughout the *Ethics*. Nevertheless, it is not difficult to imagine a limit case. What happens when there is a conflict between one's desire to know the truth (the highest part of the rational soul) and an opportunity to make the supreme sacrifice of one's life on the battlefield? This is, of course, the classic problem posed by the conflicting demands of philosophy and the city. The only point I wish to make in the present context is that Aristotle's argument for the compatibility of self-love and love of friends and fatherland or, as it is more typically framed, between egoism and altruism, in no way precludes exceptions. The problematic relationship between the philosopher and the city is neither solved nor denied by this argument. It is, however, eclipsed. Aristotle accomplishes this by appealing to the loftiest sensibilities of morally serious persons, their attraction to and capacity for the noble.

Although Aristotle does not emphasize the limitations inherent in the approach he has adopted, his analysis does bring to light a surprising rank order among the various goods discussed in this chapter. Neither love for friends nor love for the city is primary; proper or true self-love is and, by right, ought to be the central characteristic of the morally serious person.[18] Aristotle makes this point without in any way denigrating friendship or the city. On the contrary, he is characteristically sensitive to the legitimate demands that each makes on the attention of decent persons and emphasizes the extent to which proper self-love leads to appropriate and generous action on behalf of friends and fellow citizens. Paradoxically, it is by loving oneself most of all, that one is best able to benefit friends and country.

The argument of this chapter lays bare a fundamental aspect of the experience of decent persons. Proper self-love is the most appropriate basis for friendship and civic duty. Love for friends and fatherland turns out to be derivative; it is dependent upon a more natural and primary love for oneself, particularly the best part of oneself. Aristotle maintains that intelligence (*nous*) always chooses the best for itself and decent persons "obey intelligence" (*peitharchei tōi nōi*) (9.8.1169a17–18). If self-lovers in the ordinary and reprehensible sense would be improved by conforming themselves to the more exacting demands of friendship and the city, the truest lover of self recognizes in intelligence a higher and more natural standard, one that in some sense governs one's relations with friends and fellow citizens.

## FRIENDSHIP, HAPPINESS, AND PHILOSOPHY

The issues of pleasure, happiness, and the theoretical life that are addressed thematically in Book X move increasingly into the foreground in the concluding chapters on friendship (chs. 9–12). The following discussion isolates three arguments in which Aristotle foreshadows his final elevation of the theoretical life by bringing to light those aspects of friendship that are most akin to the contemplative activity of the philosopher.

The treatment of friendship gradually ascends to an explicit consideration of the guiding principle of the *Ethics* as a whole. Several arguments are made to demonstrate that friendship is essential for human happiness (9.9.1169b2–70b19). Central among them is a complex thesis that begins with the observation that human beings are better able to contemplate (*theōrein*) their neighbor's actions than their own. Beholding the deeds of friends affords a higher degree of happiness than the activity of morally serious persons without friends. Although the activity of decent persons is pleasant in itself, the pleasures of contemplation are better. Looking upon the noble deeds of a friend enables one to behold actions that are both pleasant in themselves (because good), and in some sense one's own, insofar as a friend is "another self." Even for one actively engaged in the affairs of the city, the experience of friendship provides some basis for understanding and reflecting upon the supreme happiness attaching to the more fully contemplative activity of the philosopher.

As Aristotle develops this argument, he turns once again to the perspective of natural philosophy (9.9.1170a13–70b19). In all cases, both human and nonhuman, potential becomes fully present through activity. Whereas the life of nonhuman animals is determined with reference to the activity of perception, human life involves the activities of both perceiving and thinking (*noēseōs*). For human beings, the activity of living is not only pleasant in itself but is actualized most fully when friends live together and share discussion and thought (*suzēn kai koinōnein logōn kai dianoias*) (9.9.1170b10–12). It is precisely this shared activity of discussion and thought that distinguishes the human form of association from the collective activity of nonhuman animals.

Aristotle's consideration of the importance of friendship for human happiness ascends from the contemplation of noble deeds (*praxeis*) to the more intrinsically contemplative activities of intelligence. Although these latter activities are especially prominent in philosophic friendships, there is nothing in the discussion that requires or even implies that it is exclusive to such friendships. In fact, the concluding contrast between human forms of association and nonhuman animal collectivity suggests that this culminating description of friendship extends more broadly to human beings as such. Aristotle holds up the shared life of discussion and thought as a pinnacle of human friendship and happiness that is accessible to philosopher and nonphilosopher alike.

It is worth taking stock of two additional arguments that Aristotle brings to bear on friendship since each is later used to advance his concluding thesis on the superiority of the philosophic life. The first of these is part of his general analysis of friendship and human happiness (9.9.1170a4–13). It is harder to sustain activity by oneself than it is with the aid and encouragement of others. Friendship is necessary for the fullest experience of happiness because the intrinsically pleasant activity of good persons becomes more continuous (*sunechestera*) if it is shared with friends. The inevitable waning of solitary activity due to fatigue, lack of attention, or discouragement is enhanced and supplemented by sharing that activity with friends. Aristotle argues that friendship increases an individual's capacity for activity in general and, more particularly, the activity or activities that constitute happiness. The second argument of note occurs in response to a question (9.11.1171a21–71b28). Are friends more needed in prosperity or adversity? Aristotle addresses this question by pointing to the value of friends in both circumstances. As part of his response, he maintains that in times of good fortune, the presence of friends enhances the pleasure of leisure (*diagōgē*) (9.11.1171b12–14).

Each of these two arguments on behalf of friendship directly anticipates an argument that Aristotle applies to the contemplative life in Book X. As we shall see, when Aristotle provides reasons for his concluding assessment of happiness, he maintains that the contemplative activity is both more continuous and more expressive of leisure than the activity of moral virtue (10.7.1177a21–22; 10.7.1177b4–26). By using these arguments in the present context to shed light on an activity that falls within the compass of the primary audience of the *Ethics*, Aristotle is likely to gain a more sympathetic hearing when he employs them again to advance a thesis about a way of life that, at its peak, falls outside the experience of the bulk of his readers.

Aristotle's treatment of friendship in Books VIII and IX reveals an aspect of decent experience that surpasses both moral virtue and the city in rank and dignity. By reflecting on the natural, pleasant, private, and contemplative aspects of friendship, Aristotle has, in the measure possible, prepared readers for his concluding endorsement of the rare but simply best way of life available to human beings. His subsequent demotion of the life of moral virtue in light of the superior happiness afforded by the contemplative pleasures of philosophy is perhaps less strange and less jarring because it is prefaced with a consideration of friendship.

## CHAPTER FIVE

# Making the City Safe for Philosophy, Book X

It is only in the final book of his treatise that Aristotle explicitly presents a teaching that he has intimated in different ways at various points in his study: Complete or perfect happiness is to be found in the philosophic activity of contemplation; the practice of ethical virtue is happy in a secondary degree (10.7.1177a12–18; 10.8.1178a9–10). The discussion that follows traces the rhetorical dimension of this final assessment of the relative standing of philosophic and ethical excellence by focusing on the artfulness of the argument in the concluding book of the *Ethics*. I will attempt to demonstrate that the harshness of this conclusion is mitigated by the rhetorical framework within which it has been placed. The inquiry in Book X proceeds through four themes: pleasure, happiness, the best way of life, and the turn to politics, each of which is considered in sequence.

### PLEASURE AND MORAL EDUCATION

Scholars have long recognized discrepancies in the double treatment of pleasure (7.11–14; 10.1–5) but, for the most part, have neglected to observe the very different horizons within which these two accounts are offered. As we have already observed, the initial treatment of pleasure in Book VII began by recommending it as a subject worthy of study for political philosophers (7.11.1152b1–3). This contrasts sharply with the didactic concern that guides the second consideration in Book X (10.1.1172a19–25). The subject of pleasure is reintroduced because of its critical influence on the moral education of the young. Pleasure and pain extend throughout the whole of life and are of particular import for the development of virtue and the attainment of happiness.

The approach to pleasure in Book X is consistent with Aristotle's approach to the study of ethical virtue as a whole. He mediates a debate between two extreme and influential positions with a view to directing his readers toward a salutary mean. On the one hand, Eudoxus taught that pleasure was the good, a philosophic stance that gained acceptance because it was combined with a personal reputation for exceptional moderation. Eudoxus did not appear to advocate this view because he wished to indulge in pleasure and, as a result, people assumed that he must be speaking the truth. Aristotle comments that the influence of Eudoxus's position was, however, more a reflection of his good character than the quality of his arguments (10.2.1172b16–17). On the other hand, Speussipus and members of the Academy maintained that pleasure was entirely base. Among those who adopted this second position, some really believed it to be true, whereas others maintained this view because they wanted to encourage the practice of virtue. They argued that the natural inclination toward pleasure among human beings makes it advisable to point most persons in the opposite direction, with the hope that this will bring them closer to the mean.

Aristotle takes issue with this approach, not with its aim (10.1. 1172a33–b7). He explains that in matters involving feeling and action, a particular theory or position is despised or dismissed whenever it appears to be inconsistent with the most readily perceived facts. If those who condemn pleasure are, even on occasion, seen to enjoy it, their arguments become implausible because it is assumed that, contrary to their stated position, they really believe pleasure to be the good. The arguments are discredited not necessarily because they are untrue, but because most (*hoi polloi*) lack the capacity to discriminate (*to diorizein*). For most human beings, actions speak louder than words. A further consequence is that the truth itself is undermined because of the loss of credibility occasioned by the deeds of those who may in fact be speaking it. Hence, to the extent that it is possible to bring theory into harmony with practice, the theories in question will prove more useful for the conduct of life. This practical aim characterizes Aristotle's reconsideration of pleasure in Book X and distinguishes it from his more theoretical treatment in Book VII. His attempt to harmonize theory and practice is intended to "encourage" (*protrepō*) those capable of understanding ethical arguments to live better lives (10.1.1172b3–7). A reconsideration of pleasure is made necessary by a concern for the education of decent, although not necessarily philosophic, readers.


## ARISTOTLE'S NEW DESCRIPTION OF PLEASURE

Aristotle lists the particular arguments used by Eudoxus and members of the Academy to support their respective positions, and in most cases supplies an immediate rejoinder (chs. 2–3).[1] He then goes on to offer an account of his own (chs. 4–5). The following summary focuses on those aspects of the treatment of pleasure in Book X that distinguish it most sharply from the earlier account in Book VII.

In Book VII, Aristotle defines pleasure as "unimpeded activity" and leaves open the possibility that pleasure is both the highest good and something divine. Book X offers not so much a redefinition as a new description of pleasure. Pleasure "perfects" or "completes" (teleiō) activity (10.4.1174b23). The activities of both sense perception and thought have corresponding pleasures that become most acute when the activity is executed in the best possible way. These pleasures do not inhere in the activities themselves, but rather "come to be in addition" (epigignomenon) (10.4.1174b31–33). Pleasure is a kind of unlooked for bonus that enhances activity, perfecting and increasing the capacity for action. In this new view, pleasure belongs to or depends upon activity. In Book VII, pleasure is defined as activity of a certain kind. In Book X, while maintaining that pleasure and activity are inextricably bound together, Aristotle indicates that they are nevertheless distinct. The consequences of this key difference in the two treatments of pleasure will become increasingly apparent.

The most immediate and primary corollary to follow from the new distinction is that it makes possible an independent standard by which pleasures can be ranked and judged. Activity, not pleasure, is the fundamental thing, for the latter depends upon the former. On this basis, Aristotle is able to bolster a widespread opinion among the decent that pleasure is good but not the only or supreme good. If pleasure comes from or belongs to activity, the supreme good cannot be pleasure; rather, it would belong to the best activity. With the help of this distinction, readers are now provided with edifying explanations for some of the more strident suggestions and puzzles raised by the discussion in Book VII.

Aristotle begins by returning to the question with which he had concluded his account of pleasure in Book VII: Why is it that no one is able to feel pleasure continuously (10.4.1175a3–10)? He now points out that no human faculty is characterized by uninterrupted activity, an observation that he illustrates with the example of sight. The pleasure enjoyed in seeing something depends upon looking at it intently. As the activity of looking becomes less vigorous and attention relaxes, the pleasure also fades. Book VII had emphasized an absolute limit to pleasure imposed by the composite nature of human being, a limit that emerged by means of a contrast with the single simple pleasure enjoyed perpetually by god. This teaching is not retracted in the present context, although the emphasis is different: pleasure increases or decreases in the measure that one increases or decreases effort with respect to the activity from which the pleasure arises. In a book that is intended to encourage readers to take pleasure in what they ought, Aristotle's example implies that the effort necessary for excellence in any activity is not without a certain bonus in pleasure.

He next turns his attention to the initial observation of Book X; namely, that pleasure and pain extend throughout the whole of human life (10.4.1175a12–21). It turns out that human beings have good reason to pursue pleasure, for this perfects activities and, therefore, life itself. The musician and the lover of learning are given as examples. The activity of each one is sharpened, prolonged, and improved by the pleasure that belongs to that activity. Hence, pleasure perfects the life of each one by making a person a better musician or philosopher. The argument concludes with the assertion that, for the present, we ought to dismiss the question whether life is for the sake of pleasure or pleasure for the sake of life (10.4.1175a18–19). Whatever the answer, pleasure and life appear to be inseparably yoked together (*suzeugnumi*);[2] for pleasure does not exist apart from activity, nor is there perfect activity without pleasure (10.4.1175a19–21).

It is especially in the next stages of the argument that the practical consequences of the new description of pleasure become most apparent. In contrast to an earlier puzzling suggestion that all might actually seek a single pleasure, the distinction between pleasure and activity in Book X is used to explain that pleasures differ in kind (10.5.1175a21–76a29). It is because activities differ in kind that the pleasures that belong to and augment them are seen to differ as well. In fact, pleasures derived from one activity can impede other activities. Someone may be distracted from philosophy by hearing music if the latter activity is

more pleasurable. This leads to reflection upon the vast array of pleasures arising from the multiplicity of activities undertaken by different
species of animals. If some maintain that each species has its own
proper pleasure corresponding to its particular work or activity
(10.5.1176a3–9), this view cannot be applied in an unqualified way to
the human species (10.5.1176a10–29). Human beings enjoy a bewildering variety of pleasures. Some indication of the problem is evidenced by
the fact that the same things delight some people and cause pain to others. Feverish and healthy persons find different things to be sweet, and
the same temperature is both painful and pleasant to the weak and the
robust. The more serious difficulty, however, concerns the different
kinds of pleasure sought out and cultivated by human beings. The three
most conspicuous have been anticipated since the outset of the *Ethics*,
namely, the different kinds of pleasures connected with the senses, with
honors and political offices, and, less frequently but no less emphatically, with study. How is one to find an appropriate standard by which
to rank these pleasures? Given the variation and irregularity that characterizes human affairs, is it even possible to speak of a distinctively
human pleasure?

It is here that the ethical bearing of the distinction between pleasure
and activity becomes explicit (10.5.1175b24–29). Since activity is the
fundamental thing, it is possible not only to distinguish various pleasures, but to do so by determining the moral worth of the activities to
which they correspond. On the basis of this distinction, pleasures
accompanying morally serious activities (*spoudaiai*) are differentiated
from those that are base (*phauloi*). In all cases, the thing is as it appears
to the morally serious person (*ho spoudaios*) (10.5.1176a15–16). Moreover, if we wish to know what constitutes the distinctively human pleasure or pleasures, we should look to the best activity or activities of "the
perfect and blessed man" (*tou teleiou kai makariou andros*). All other
pleasures sought by human beings are "human" in secondary and even
more tenuous ways, depending upon the activities from which they
arise (10.5.1176a24–29).

More precisely, Aristotle writes that the perfect and blessed person
reveals the pleasure or pleasures that are human in the most authoritative (*kuriōs*) sense, that other pleasures are human in a secondary (*deuterōs*) degree, and still others are even more remotely (*pollostōs*) connected with distinctively human activity (10.5.1176a26–29). Although
*deuterōs kai pollostōs* is sometimes taken as a single idiomatic expression, it is helpful to call attention to the distinct meanings of these

adverbs. Taken literally, this passage articulates the threefold hierarchy that provides the rhetorical framework for the argument of Book X. Aristotle's distinctions between primary, secondary, and remotely human pleasures correspond to the three views of happiness that he had introduced in Book I and to which he is about to return. The life of study, the moral-political life, and the life devoted to sensual pleasure are each given their proper weight as the *Ethics* approaches its denouement.

Before turning to the final thematic treatment of happiness, we should not allow a persistent ambiguity to pass without comment: Who, precisely, is the morally serious human being? Is Aristotle thinking of the magnanimous person or the philosopher when he speaks of the perfect and blessed person? Despite the obvious importance of this question, Aristotle has not at this point provided his readers with a definitive answer. He does not even call attention to the question; rather, he seems intent upon retaining a certain ambiguity. Indeed, such ambiguity is not without practical effect, since it is apt to elicit greater openness on the part of decent readers who are able and likely to find in these expressions recognition of the fact that they do, or at least should, provide the standard for all who fall below them. Such a reading is not incorrect but, as will become clear in the sequel, it is incomplete.


## HAPPINESS AND THE PLEASURES OF THE POWERFUL

Whereas Book I provided an outline or sketch of the relationship between happiness and ethical virtue, Book X returns to this subject in a thematic way. It begins by recapitulating some of the initial conclusions about happiness from Book I (10.6.1176a30–76b9). Happiness is not a disposition, but some form of activity that is chosen for its own sake and is lacking in nothing. This way of describing happiness is also believed to describe the nature of virtuous actions, since noble and virtuous deeds are desirable for their own sake. The implicit identification of happiness and ethical virtue is taken over from Book I and constitutes the perspective that, with a few notable exceptions, has been adopted and clarified throughout the study. Only in Book X does Aristotle address in a serious way a problem that challenges the special or authoritative status such a view confers on morally serious persons. The pleasures of play also appear to be desirable for their own sake (10.6.1176b9–17).[3] So simple an assertion is not so simply dismissed.

Not only are such amusements thought by many (*hoi polloi*) to constitute happiness; but also and especially, those in positions of absolute power (*turannoi*) are seen to devote themselves to such pastimes. The life styles of the rich and famous undermine the meritorious belief that happiness is to be found in the morally serious activities of decent human beings.[4]

Aristotle responds with five arguments, all of which demonstrate the unique capacity of philosophy to defend and clarify the dignity of moral virtue despite the weight of actual political practice (10.6. 1176b17–77a11): (1) It is a lack of experience in mature pleasures that leads many, like children, to think that more accessible but lesser pleasures are best. (2) The serious work that fills human life is not for the sake of fleeting moments of play. Rather, the opposite is the case; play is a form of rest that is for the sake of further activity. (3) In the measure that happiness requires virtue, it will be found in serious activities rather than amusements. (4) Things that are taken seriously are better than funny or amusing things, and happiness engages the better part of the soul. (5) The fact that no one would deem slaves happy despite their ability to enjoy bodily pleasures indicates that happiness involves activities of a different kind.

Each of these five arguments advances the claim that the example of the powerful should be judged by a more authoritative standard furnished by the activities of morally serious persons. The particular arguments used to reinforce this claim are prefaced with a general statement that reveals something of the strategy employed in this section as a whole. Since virtue (*aretē*) and intelligence (*nous*) give rise to the most pure (*eilikrinēs*) and liberal (*eleutherios*) pleasures, happiness cannot consist in the pleasures of play, but in activities in accordance with the virtue and intelligence of morally serious persons (10.6.1176b18–28).

The arguments in this section combine the natural standard of pleasure with a standard furnished by decent opinion. Aristotle does this in two ways. First, he relies on the earlier distinction between pleasure and activity to rule out a priori the possibility that pleasure could provide an independent standard for human conduct. It should be noticed, however, that the claim that pleasure furnishes such a standard is reflected in the pastime activities of the powerful. Second, by including both virtue and intelligence within the single category of activities that give rise to pure and liberal pleasures, Aristotle does not call attention to the ambiguous meaning of these words. Virtue (*aretē*) explicitly embraces both ethical and intellectual excellence, and although intelligence (*nous*), strictly speaking, designates a theoretical activity, it has also been used, as we have seen, to refer to the activity of practical reason as well. Aristotle minimizes the extent to which different activities falling within the categories of *aretē* and *nous*, and the pleasures arising from them, can lead to radically different ways of life.[5] There is, of course, some warrant for this conflation, since, as the discussion of intellectual excellence in Book VI has already made apparent, the life of ethical virtue also involves reason.[6] Aristotle's argument in the present context is consistent with his earlier lack of precision in this matter. Instead of emphasizing that the activities of virtue and intelligence can lead to two different ways of life, he uses both as attributes to describe the activity of the "morally serious person," an expression that is itself laden with ambiguity.

The argument effectively forges an alliance between the philosopher and the nonphilosopher. They are united in opposing the opinion of the many and even the authority of sovereigns who, by their example, teach that happiness consists in the pleasures of play. Morally decent persons possess greater authority on this issue than the rich and famous because they experience pleasures that are purer, more liberal, more serious, and, in general, more specifically human, than those typically desired by the many and indulged by the powerful.

## HAPPINESS AND THE BEST WAY OF LIFE

It is only after eliciting this sense of solidarity among morally serious persons that Aristotle clarifies the exact relationship between ethical and intellectual excellence as it bears on the all-important question of happiness. As we have anticipated, the final book of the *Ethics* confronts its readers with a surprising demotion of moral virtue in light of the superior happiness of the contemplative life. If happiness consists in activity in accordance with virtue, it is reasonable that it should be activity in accordance with the best virtue. Unlike his initial and open-ended presentation of this argument in Book I (1.7.1098a16–18), Aristotle now specifies that the best and most perfect virtue consists in the godlike activity of contemplation. Happiness is coextensive in its range with contemplative excellence; the exercise of moral virtue is happy in a secondary way (10.7.1177a12–18; 10.8.1178b28–32; 10.8.1178a9–10).

This conclusion, in some way the culmination of the entire book, is oddly out of step with the rest of Aristotle's study. It is incompatible

with the earlier and dominant teaching of the *Ethics*, one that emphasized the intrinsic value of both moral virtue and friendship for a flourishing human life. Moreover, apart from the dissonances of which the
reader of this book is especially aware, this conclusion is in large measure unanticipated. The prominence given in Aristotle's treatise tò both
excellences of character (Bks. II–V) and friendship (Bks. VIII–IX) leads
more readily to the conclusion that human happiness is a composite of
activities involving character, friendship, and reflection. This expected
conclusion is, however, unexpectedly derailed by Aristotle's elevation of
the theoretical life and subsequent deflation of moral virtue.

The incongruent character of the conclusion of the *Ethics* returns
us to the starting point for the current study. The apparent incompati-
bility of X.7–8 with the rest of the treatise has led scholars to the various
critical assessments summarized in chapter 1. As should by now be
clear, I do not think it is necessary to conclude that the *Ethics* is marred
by a fundamental incoherence or that the arguments of X.7–8 have been
carelessly grafted onto the trunk of the *Ethics* by Aristotle or a later edi-
tor. Rather, these chapters espouse a position that has in fact been
present throughout the entire study, with two notable differences. First,
whereas this argument has been kept in the background as an alternative to the dominant teaching of the *Ethics*, it is now given a position of
preeminence. Indeed, it is made into the climax of the book as a whole.
Secondly, as we shall see, this shift is accompanied by another. Aristotle's most explicit endorsement of the philosophic life mutes rather than
emphasizes the extent to which a life devoted to philosophic inquiry
conflicts radically with the demands of moral-political excellence. This,
I shall argue, is achieved by presenting a beautiful, if rarified, image of
philosophic activity that is in important respects both similar and complementary to the moral-political excellence of the *kalos k'agathos*.

Aristotle's concluding teaching on the surpassing happiness of the
philosophic life is supported by six arguments (10.7.1177a18–b26): (1)
Contemplation is the best (*kratistē*) activity because it involves the best
thing in us. (2) It is the most continuous activity in which human beings
can engage. (3) It is held to contain pleasures of marvelous purity and
permanence. (4) It is the most self-sufficient activity, for the wise need
not depend upon others in order to contemplate. (5) It is loved for its
own sake and produces no result beyond itself. (6) It is an activity of leisure par excellence. On the basis of these six arguments, Aristotle concludes that contemplation is the highest activity in accordance with virtue and, consequently, that complete human happiness consists in a life

of study. He also anticipates the objection that such a life exceeds human capacity (10.7.1177b26–78a2). If the intellect (*nous*) is something divine in comparison to human capacity, then the life of the intellect would describe a divine, not a human, life. Against this objection, Aristotle urges that we must not follow those who enjoin that mortals should have thoughts of mortality. Rather, as far as possible, we ought to be immortal, and do all that we can to live in accordance with the best thing in us. In sharp contrast to the sober teaching of Book VII on the composite nature of human being, Aristotle concludes his study with a seemingly Platonic exhortation to cultivate the most divine aspect of the human soul. Human happiness is not identified with a range of activities reflecting the composite nature of human being but with the most godlike activity of which human beings are capable.

The argument of these chapters invokes a conception of philosophic activity that stands in sharp contrast to the understanding of political philosophy that Aristotle has discretely but persistently exhibited throughout his study. It suffices to recall the more jarring aspects of his teaching to bring this difference into full view. In the course of his inquiry, Aristotle has suggested the dependence of ethical virtue on *orthos logos*, the circular or ungrounded character of prudence from which *orthos logos* arises, persistent and unresolved tensions between different peaks of ethical excellence (most notably magnanimity and justice), the instrumental character of prudence for the attainment of wisdom, the possibility that pleasure could be the highest good, and the nature and limits of friendship in light of a necessary concern with self-love. I have emphasized the extent to which Aristotle's consideration of each of these issues is left deliberately open ended. It would be inaccurate to confer the status of 'ethical doctrine" upon any of these points. Quite the contrary, it is the intractable character of these problems that reveals, in a way that has yet to be fully appreciated, the essentially dialectical ground in which Aristotle's more familiar ethical and political doctrines are embedded.

In contrast to the kind of political philosophy exhibited in Aristotle's text, his concluding endorsement of philosophy is tame.[7] The final image of philosophic activity is idealized in the sense that it is removed from, and therefore less apparently in conflict with, the exigencies of moral and political life. Philosophy is presented as a thing apart, a godlike activity that does not threaten decent sensibilities because it is not preoccupied with the necessities that constrain civic life. Aristotle's final teaching about the dignity of the philosophic life reflects his concern for nonphilosophic readers: His most explicit endorsement of the surpass-ing value of contemplation extols a domesticated version of philosophy, one in which philosophic activity is reduced to a largely private or aca-demic enterprise, shorn of the unwieldy and disruptive political conse-quences that inevitably attend a life of radical inquiry.

Aristotle's arguments for the superiority of the philosophic life con-front readers in an unambiguous way with a truth that many of them would necessarily find disconcerting. However, unlike Platonic ver-sions of this teaching, which are almost invariably met by anger or rid-icule on the part of Socrates' interlocutors, Aristotle has reason to expect that his presentation of the dignity of the philosophic life will be neither dismissed nor ridiculed by the majority of his nonphilosophic readers. Not only has he painstakingly clarified the horizon of ethical virtue on its own terms in the first half of the *Ethics* and pointed to a relatively innocuous version of theoretical excellence in the concluding chapters of his study, but, as we shall see, even this most explicit teach-ing on the superiority of the philosophic life is offered within a broader context that emphasizes the similar and even complementary character of ethical and intellectual virtue.

## ONE CONSISTENT TEACHING:
## SIMILAR AND COMPLEMENTARY WAYS OF LIFE

The similarity between philosophic and ethical excellence is suggested by the particular arguments used to establish the superior happiness of the contemplative life. All six of these arguments apply, to some extent at least, to ethical excellence as well. It is possible to argue that a life characterized by the practice of ethical virtue is superior to, and happier than, a life given over to the enjoyment of bodily pleasures and amuse-ments, the example of sovereigns notwithstanding, for precisely the rea-sons used to demonstrate the ultimate superiority of the philosophic life.

These arguments, or variants of them, are in fact applied by Aristotle to ethical virtue. With respect to the six propositions enumerated above, one should consider the following Aristotelian assertions: (1) Justice is considered the best (*kratistē*) of the virtues (5.1.1129b27–28). (2) Friend-ship, based on the practice of moral virtue, facilitates the continuous activity characteristic of happiness (9.9.1170a5–11). (3) Pure and liberal pleasures are found in the activities of virtue and intelligence (10.6.

1176b18–21). Less broadly, generosity in particular and virtuous action in general are accompanied by pleasure (4.1.1120a24–31). (4) Self-suf-ficiency is characteristic of the magnanimous person (4.3.1125a11–12). (5) The repeated insistence that noble actions are desirable for their own sake is one of the leitmotifs of the *Ethics* (e.g., 3.7.1115b11–13; 4.1. 1120a23–25; 4.2.1122b6–7; 10.6.1176b6–9). (6) Justice and moderation are cited as activities appropriate to leisure (*Pol.* 7.15.1334a11–34).

The reason for calling attention to these statements is not to ques-tion Aristotle's final evaluation of the theoretical life. Rather, it is to make clear that the very arguments used to substantiate its superiority simultaneously suggest a similarity between philosophic and moral excellence. The philosophic life is happier than the moral life not because it is radically different from it, but because it offers to a greater and more perfect degree the very things that decent persons both seek and enjoy for themselves. It is within the broader framework of several propositions bearing on both philosophic and moral excellence that Aristotle presents his most explicit teaching on the superiority of the philosophic life.

This affirmation of the superiority of contemplative excellence necessitates some further consideration of ethical virtue. The issue is confronted in chapter 8, where ethical virtue is also said to result in hap-piness, but in some lesser way than the godlike activity of philosophic contemplation. However, as we shall see, the argument of this chapter as a whole also suggests that ethical and intellectual virtues are not mutually exclusive but rather complementary forms of excellence for human beings.

Moral virtue is reduced to a secondary rank because it is an activity limited by a need for, and dependence upon, others (10.8.1178a9–b7). By way of contrast, the happiness of contemplation requires less "external equipment," an expression that, in Aristotle's usage, includes other human beings. In fact, the kind of equipment necessary for doing virtuous deeds, especially great ones, might in some cases prove to be a hindrance to contemplation (10.8.1178b1–5). If this argument is more forthcoming about a dissimilarity and possible tension between the moral and contemplative ways of life, such candor is immediately restrained by asserting that the philosopher, since he lives in society, also chooses to engage in virtuous actions (10.8. 1178b5–7).

If, as Aristotle has argued in the preceding chapter, morally decent persons ought to look up to the philosopher as the exemplar of the best way of life, he now indicates that the philosopher is not, or at least should not be, indifferent to the moral-political concerns that are the special preoccupation of the city and those who bear primary responsibility for its welfare. The philosopher is human (*anthrōpeuesthai*) and for that reason needs to live among other human beings (10.8.1178b5–7; see 7.14.1154b20–31). We are thus brought to consider the possibility of a complementary relationship between theoretical and moral virtue. Whereas the life of the philosopher discloses the fullest possibility of happiness for human beings, morally decent persons embody the kind of excellence necessary to live well in the polis. The two kinds of excellence complement each other because of the essentially political character of composite beings who are able to appreciate but not sustain godlike simplicity.

Although ethical virtue is reduced to a secondary status because of its dependence upon external goods, Aristotle's final argument on this subject softens without denying this diminution (10.8.1178b33–79a9). Since human nature is not self-sufficient with respect to contemplation, even philosophers must concern themselves with external well-being. However, as the life of philosophy reveals, happiness does not require an abundance of external goods. In this respect, it is possible for the practitioner of moral virtue to imitate the philosopher, since one can also undertake virtuous actions with modest resources. It is possible, Aristotle writes, to do noble deeds without being a ruler of land and sea (10.8.1179a4–5). Indeed, he observes that private citizens are more likely to act in accord with the requirements of virtue than those in positions of political authority. This conclusion is supported by drawing from the sayings of Solon and Anaxagoras—a wise statesman and a philosopher (10.8.1179a9–17). Both citations give added authority to the final edifying teaching of the *Ethics* on happiness: Contrary to what most believe, happiness is not to be found in the excesses of the powerful but rather in imitating, as much as possible, the materially unencumbered activity of philosophers.[8]

This emphasis on the similar and complementary character of ethical and philosophic excellence points to a single consistent teaching on the best life for a human being. The argument suggests that ethical and philosophic excellence, though distinct, are not incompatible. The tentative character of the argument in Book I gives way to greater, though still incomplete, specificity in Book X. The happiness of each individual, nonphilosopher and potential philosopher alike, depends upon the full development of the soul, a development that gives first but not exclusive priority to whatever theoretical capacity one might possess. The reader is led to conclude that one should give paramount importance to the life of study, depending upon ability and circumstances, while at the same time developing the more generally accessible ethical virtues.


## TWO INCONSISTENT TEACHINGS:
## PERSISTENT TENSION

We should, however, be careful to observe that although Aristotle does not emphasize dissimilarity or dissonance in the relationship between ethical and theoretical virtue in Book X, neither does he deny it.[9] Indeed, he weaves into the argument of his concluding book three striking indications of persistent tension: (1) the unanswered question whether life is for the sake of pleasure (10.4.1175a18–19), (2) the suggestion that the practice of the greatest and most noble moral virtues impedes the highest human excellence (10.8.1178b1–5), and (3) the apparently insignificant character of moral virtue in light of divine activity (10.8.1178b7–23). Each of these passages is briefly discussed below.

(1) As we have already noted, in the course of his reconsideration of pleasure, Aristotle raises a crucial theoretical question: Is life for the sake of pleasure or pleasure for the sake of life? Gauthier and Jolif point out that the decision to put this question aside as inappropriate in the present context has occasioned a great deal of comment on the part of those who are uncomfortable with Aristotle's willingness to turn away from such a crucial issue. They observe that most major commentators (Alexander of Aphrodisias, Michael of Ephesus, St. Albert, St. Thomas, et al.) have not been able to resist the temptation to try to resolve a question that the text leaves in suspense. Gauthier and Jolif, finding some support in Burnet, proceed to argue that such efforts are misguided since, whatever the answer to this question, Aristotle is here arguing that the contemplative "activity-pleasure" (*le bloc opération-plaisir*) constitutes the ultimate end for human beings.[10] Although they are surely correct in maintaining that this constitutes the overall argument in Book X, their explanation does not adequately account for the passage in question, which explicitly raises the question whether life is for the sake of pleasure or pleasure for the sake of life. The discomfort of earlier commentators seems more justified than the effort to minimize a deliberately open-ended

question by subordinating it to the most obvious conclusion of the *Ethics* as a whole.

The dismissal of a question that he has nevertheless put into the minds of his readers in some sense draws attention to the question itself and, in so doing, to the central difference between Books VII and X. What constitutes the fundamental standard for human beings? Is it pleasure or a kind of life that is characterized by noble disregard for questions of this sort? The disturbing character of Aristotle's failure to resolve this question in the concluding book of the *Ethics* is augmented by the fact that he had earlier cited with apparent approval, the belief that nothing prevents pleasure from being the supreme good (7.13. 1153b7–8), a view that implies that life is for the sake of pleasure. Without going so far as to suggest that Aristotle advocates a kind of philosophic hedonism, it is sufficient to observe that the unanswered question about pleasure in Book X, together with the arguments from Book VII (11–14) that it recalls, evidences the continuing presence of a perspective that is alien to the teaching on ethical virtue for which the *Ethics* is rightly famous.

(2)  In his final discussion of happiness, Aristotle suggests that the external equipment necessary for great and noble actions may constitute an impediment to the life of study (10.8.1178b1–5). Although he does not elaborate the problem here, it is easily clarified in light of his earlier discussions. Peak moral virtues such as magnificence and magnanimity presuppose an abundance of external goods, something that in turn requires attentiveness to the economic and political circumstances that make these virtues possible and appropriate. A preoccupation with these concerns and with the constantly shifting circumstances from which they arise reduces both suitability and appreciation for a life given over to the contemplation of the unchanging beings of nature.

Moreover, whereas the pleasure associated with each activity enhances that activity, it has the further effect of impeding other activities (10.5.1175a29–b24). Given the morally edifying horizon that prevails in Book X, it is not surprising that Aristotle fails to apply this principle directly to the different activities of ethical and philosophic excellence. He restricts himself to the considerably less controversial observation that the pleasures arising from musical harmony can be an obstacle to the activity of philosophy. It is, however, difficult to imagine that someone who has experienced the nearly divine pleasures of contemplation would not find the pleasures associated with ethical virtue to be in some respect diminished.[11]

(3) In the course of his final assessment of ethical virtue, Aristotle turns once again to the question of divine activity (10.8.1178b7–23). It is here that the problematic relationship between ethical and intellectual virtue becomes most apparent. In what does the happiness of the gods consist? It would be ludicrous to try to conceive of them as practicing moral virtue, since all forms of virtuous conduct are "trifling and unworthy" (*mikra kai anaxia*) of gods (10.8.1178b17–18). The only possible activity appropriate to deities is some form of contemplation. This description of the gods, one that echoes the earlier account in Book VII (7.14.1154b26–31), is Aristotle's most severe and most explicit criticism of the human tendency to project a concern for ethical virtue onto the divine. He argues instead that happiness is coextensive in its range with contemplation (10.8.1178b28–32). Given the essentially political character of human beings, human imitation of divine indifference toward moral virtue would be reprehensible. Nevertheless, an appropriate human approximation of divine detachment expresses itself in the cultivation of ethical virtue as a means to the godlike activity of contemplation, not as an end in itself.

By way of contrast, the happiness of the *kalos k'agathos* is limited, not only by a need for those external goods necessary for the practice of moral virtue, but because the most sublime happiness turns out to belong to another kind of activity. Aristotle's depiction of divine disinterestedness, together with his identification of human happiness and the godlike activity of contemplation, points to the existence of a still unresolved tension between ethical and philosophic excellence. This problem is exacerbated by Aristotle's further undeveloped suggestion that the activity of *nous*, more than anything else, constitutes the identity of a human being (10.7.1178a5–8), a suggestion that undercuts his earlier insistence on the composite nature of human being as the most salient aspect of human identity and therefore happiness.

Whereas the dominant argument of Book X establishes the superior happiness of the philosophic life within a context emphasizing the similar and complementary character of ethical and intellectual excellence, these three brief but pointed remarks suggest that the exact relationship between them remains problematic. Those most attuned to these notes of discord are likely to detect in the *Ethics* the presence of two inconsistent teachings on the best way to live as a human being.

## CONCLUDING ARGUMENTS:
## GODS, MORAL NOBILITY, AND THE CITY

The sharpness of the conflict between the requirements and sensibilities of moral and contemplative virtue is reflected nowhere more clearly than in Aristotle's contrast between human and divine activity in Books VII and X (7.14.1154b20–31; 10.8.1178b7–23). This teaching, however, is at odds with the final argument of the *Ethics* on this subject (10.8.1179a22–29). Aristotle maintains that if, as is generally held, the gods exercise some concern over human affairs, they are likely to benefit those who most love and honor godlike excellence in themselves. Those who cultivate intelligence (*nous*) and undertake "right and noble deeds" (*orthōs te kai kalōs prattontas*) are most beloved by the gods and recompensed with godlike happiness. The premise of this argument flatly contradicts Aristotle's previous description of the gods. Divine indifference to moral virtue has given way to a more consoling preoccupation with and concern for correct and noble human actions.

The contradiction, however, does not lie in Aristotle's thinking, since this final argument about the gods is explicitly drawn from a pervasive and decent opinion rather than from Aristotle himself. Thus, without actually retracting his theoretical speculations about divine activity, he overlays them with a concluding and morally edifying argument about the gods. The gods reward those who practice moral virtue and honor intelligence. Despite the profound *theoretical* differences that separate the two portrayals of the divine in this chapter, it is important to observe that, taken together, these accounts direct readers to a single consistent *practical* teaching: One ought to imitate the gods as much as possible and, depending upon one's abilities and circumstances, this means giving a privileged place to intelligence in either its theoretical or practical manifestations. Whereas the contemplative activity of theoretical intelligence enables one to *experience* godlike happiness, Aristotle's concluding argument holds out the *promise* of such happiness to those who honor intelligence by performing noble deeds. The fulfillment of this promise depends upon the veracity of the pervasive and decent opinion about divine solicitude for human affairs. Although attentive readers might be more impressed by the distance between human and divine concerns and what that implies about the best way of life for a human being, the final reference to the gods in the *Ethics* encourages all readers to live in accordance with the best thing in them and to revere rather than disparage those who most embody the peculiar excellence of philosophic contemplation.

The concluding chapter of the *Ethics* returns to a theme that has implicitly informed the study as a whole and explicitly guided the consideration in Book X, namely, the moral education of the young. Although speech may be sufficient to encourage generous youths to pursue a life of moral nobility (*kalokagathia*), speech by itself is unlikely to awaken a similar desire in the majority of human beings (10.9. 1179b7–10). Since most are ruled by passions, compulsion and punishment are more effective than the appeal to reason and the noble (10.9. 1180a3–5). Hence, there arises a need for laws that take their bearings from moral nobility but are also backed by the strong arm of the civic body. The application of force is necessary not only for the city in that it establishes the rudiments of political order, but also and especially for individual citizens since it encourages them to live in accordance with the best thing in them.

If the argument of the preceding two chapters demotes the life of moral virtue in light of the most perfectly happy life of philosophy, the concluding chapter of the *Ethics* draws upon the broader context within which that argument has been framed. The extent to which these two ways of life are similar and complementary is most evident when they are contrasted to the lower and more pervasive alternative that dominates actual political practice. Aristotle's sober evaluation of the nature and limits of the majority of human beings directs our attention to the third component of the threefold hierarchy that has been especially prominent in Book X. Those whose lives are susceptible to the influence of reason and the noble define *orthos logos* for the majority of human beings whose lives are circumscribed by passion. Aristotle concludes his study of ethics and introduces the study of politics in a way that allows the resplendent character of moral virtue to stand together with philosophic contemplation as the authoritative standard for the laws of the city. In so doing, he emphasizes the dignity of a life characterized by the practice of moral virtue, its practical importance for politics, and the need that all those who bear primary responsibility for the city have for the philosopher, who—in the person of Aristotle—promises to help his readers gain a better understanding of the crucial relationship between virtue and actual political practice in the second half of his "philosophy concerning the human things."

## CONSISTENT INCONSISTENCY

The continuing controversy over Aristotle's teaching on the precise relationship between moral and theoretical excellence is well grounded in the text. I have attempted to show that the ambiguity of this treatment is due, at least in part, to the fact that he provides two different accounts of this relationship, a fact that is itself attributable to the different audiences to which the book is addressed.

For the majority of Aristotle's decent, reflective, but not essentially philosophic, readers, ethical virtue is presented on its own terms and with a degree of clarity and precision that is appropriate to its subject matter. Although he argues for the existence of something higher than the life of ethical virtue, the overarching teaching of Book X takes issue with the widespread human tendency to identify happiness with the pleasures of play by pointing to the greater satisfactions to be derived from the practice of moral virtue. Moreover, the emphasis on a similar and complementary relationship between ethical and philosophic excellence directs readers away from the seductive extremes of unreflective patriotism and political domination. By subordinating passion to intelligence and intelligence to contemplation, Aristotle points toward that aspect of human activity that offers the greatest possibility of happiness. Insofar as decent persons are more concerned to cultivate the life of the mind than amass money, power, and prestige, they are able to experience something of the godlike happiness of the philosopher.

To those who are most attracted to the theoretical life, Aristotle's treatment offers a second, more problematic ground for serious concern with ethical virtue. The *Ethics* urges attentiveness to the practice of moral virtue, not as an end in itself or as something that provides the greatest happiness but as a means to the end of contemplation. This argument is double edged. Whereas it is reassuring to learn that philosophers are or should be concerned about moral virtue, the argument simultaneously raises a question as to whether their motivation is consistent with the requirements of moral virtue itself.

A harsh expression of this so-called intellectualist argument is found in *Magna Moralia*, where ethical virtue is reduced to the status of a household manager who attends to daily necessities so that the lord of the house might enjoy the freedom and leisure necessary to engage in philosophic thought (*MM* 1.34.1198b9–20; see *EE* 8.3.1249b4–25). The difference between this account and the one given in the *Nicomachean Ethics* is instructive. Although both discussions clearly affirm the supe-

riority of the philosophic life, in the *Ethics* moral virtue is said to be subordinate to, but never the servant of, philosophic contemplation.
Whereas the latter view suggests that ethical virtue is ultimately devoid
of intrinsic dignity, the argument of the *Ethics* is distinctive precisely for
its insistence on an independent status for ethical virtue. Indeed, Aristotle's often-repeated assertion that moral acts are undertaken for their
own sake comes as close as any single line to constituting a refrain for
the entire book. In the *Ethics* Aristotle subordinates the life of ethical
virtue to the philosophic way of life while at the same time retaining a
sense of its importance. The life of ethical virtue, unlike the life of sla-
very, does result in substantial human happiness. Nevertheless, a still
greater possibility exists for those who are able to take their bearings
from the supremely happy activity of philosophic contemplation.

It is, I believe, a mistake to conclude that Aristotle's teaching on the
best life is inconsistent. The deeper consistency that I have attempted to
bring to light is reflected in his refusal to simplify the question of the
best way of life. His depiction of ethical virtue is faithful to the phenomenon of ethical virtue as it appears in the lives of its best exemplars. At
the same time, his account of philosophic activity preserves without
emphasizing a sense of the inevitable controversy that accompanies a
life of radical inquiry. Theoretical and practical matters vie for the
attention of human intelligence and, given the very different and necessarily limited capacities of human beings, the full development of one
can lessen appreciation for the importance of the other.[12] Aristotle consistently resists the temptation to try to reconcile completely two ele-
vated ways of life that cannot be in every respect reconciled.

The well-known conclusion of the *Ethics* regarding the superiority
of the philosophic life is shaped by a considerably less-appreciated Aristotelian concern for the character and limits of nonphilosophic readers.
Although it would be wrong to conclude from an awareness of the rhetorical dimension of his arguments that Aristotle considers those arguments to be false, it would be equally misleading to identify them in an
unqualified way with his own view of the subject. The rhetorical presentation of philosophy in the *Ethics* succeeds in muting, without actually
denying, a fundamental tension between philosophy and politics. Careful study of the concluding book of the *Ethics* provides the reader with
an example of the Aristotelian understanding of the art of rhetoric, an
art that is used not to obscure the nature of philosophy but rather to
reveal substantial, if incomplete, truths about it. If, as Aristotle maintains, Alcidamas's rhetorical claim that philosophy should be consid-

ered "a bulwark of the laws" is too exaggerated to be credible (*Rh.* 3.3.1406b5–15), Aristotle's rhetorical art is calculated to win at least a partial acceptance of philosophy on the part of those who are or will be most responsible for directing the affairs of the city.

# Conclusion

Most students of Western philosophy assume they know what Aristotle says about ethics. This confidence derives, at least in part, from the very success of Aristotle's enterprise. But, to invoke a caution with an Aristotelian resonance, success does not come without impediments. The presumption of familiarity often distances students from an author by inadvertently encouraging reliance upon conventional anthologies rather than inviting fresh appraisals of a classic text. Standard summaries of Aristotle's corpus, whatever their merits, necessarily gloss over the more perplexing and seemingly inconsistent aspects of his treatise. I have attempted to follow the argument of the *Ethics* without presuming that such passages are, in fact, a departure from the intended teaching of the book as a whole. I have also resisted the temptation to rely upon the various scholarly hypotheses developed to explain or dismiss the obvious incongruities that plague the text as it now stands. The result of these efforts has been the discovery of an Aristotle who is both more consistent and more unruly than is usually recognized.

The most traditional account of Aristotle rightly differentiates his approach to the study of ethics from that of his most famous teacher. The dependence of political virtue on the always imperfectly just aspirations of the regime led Plato to criticize, sometimes harshly, the way of life of the *kalos k'agathos*. Unlike Plato, Aristotle gives greater scope to the kind of moral and political excellence constrained by the vicissitudes of political life. Indeed, he maintains that ethical virtue possesses a certain kind of self-sufficiency, qualified to be sure, and is characterized by the high and admirable standard of reflectiveness found in the individual who embodies practical wisdom. Aristotle invests the non-philosophic way of life with unplatonic seriousness, clarifying, modifying, and even embellishing its attractiveness as the necessary and fertile ground for human experience.

However, like Plato, Aristotle is not primarily concerned with the propagation of salutary truths about human life; philosophic probity requires that he also entertain serious alternatives to the ethical precepts most typically attributed to him. Although the *Ethics* points to a godlike and seemingly apolitical version of philosophic activity in its conclusion, the study as a whole conveys a more sober and more problematic understanding of philosophy, one that concerns itself especially with political matters. Not only does Aristotle consider the rare alternative afforded by a life of radical inquiry, but he carefully, if discretely, acknowledges that it cannot be in every respect harmonized with the doctrines for which the *Ethics* is rightly famous. Aristotle demonstrates rather than recommends a way through the impasse: The practice of *political* philosophy is characterized by both a concern for politics and an awareness of something beyond politics. Rather than prescribe a formula or propose a solution, Aristotle brings to light the competing demands of two ways of life that most merit attention and effectively invites his audience—philosophers and nonphilosophers alike—to find a balance or combination appropriate to their circumstances and abilities.

Notwithstanding Hegel's well-known injunction that philosophy must guard against being edifying, the *Ethics* succeeds in being both salubrious and philosophic. Time-honored ethical principles are presented on their own terms and with the degree of clarity of which they admit. Aristotle also indicates that rigorous consideration of these principles involves readers in a thoughtful consideration of alternatives that are never entirely dismissed or reconciled with the most familiar maxims of the book. The unresolved character of these tensions, undoubtedly a source of frustration for many of Aristotle's commentators, is also a catalyst for further reflection. While textual discrepancies have given rise to charges of inconsistency, they also goad those readers most troubled by them to further reflection about the best way of life. The edifying moral-political teaching of the *Ethics* rests upon a theoretical foundation that is intractably aporetic. Aristotle's deep and insufficiently appreciated agreement with Plato on ethical matters lies in the irreducibly dialectical basis in which his account of ethical inquiry is set.

The rhetorical art of the *Ethics* is evident both in the powerful appeal of its moral-political tenets and by the way in which Aristotle discloses the aporetic character of its theoretical foundations. Plato claimed to have depicted the Socrates of the dialogues as "young and beautiful," something that is not without an Aristotelian counterpart. Throughout his study, Aristotle furnishes readers with accounts of ethical virtue, friendship, and philosophy that are both vigorous and beautiful. However, just as thoughtful study of the Platonic dialogues confronts readers with a more complex and radically disruptive Socrates, attentive study of the *Ethics* reveals the provocative and open-ended character of Aristotelian political philosophy. The ethical horizon that Aristotle elucidates and seeks to foster does not completely or fundamentally constrain his own enterprise. Rather, he exhibits an understanding of political philosophy that is marked by both a serious concern for virtue and the artful employment of rhetoric. Aristotelian political philosophy demonstrates a politically responsible way of combining sensitivity to the salutary demands of common decency with the sharp and necessarily jarring perspective characteristic of radical inquiry.

# NOTES

## INTRODUCTION

1. Numerical citations are taken from the Oxford edition and refer to the *Nicomachean Ethics* unless otherwise indicated. Unmodified references to the *Ethics* refer to the *Nicomachean Ethics*. Translations, though indebted to Rackham (1926) and Irwin (1985), are my own.

2. This same tension between words and deeds is present in the *Laches*. See Michael O'Brien, "The Unity of the *Laches*," *Yale Classical Studies* 18 (1963): 133–47; and Aristide Tessitore, "Courage and Comedy in Plato's *Laches*," *The Journal of Politics* 56 (February 1994): 115–33.

3. This sharply critical sentiment is echoed elsewhere in the Platonic dialogues. See, e.g., *Gorgias* 521a–22e; *Republic* 496a–e; *Meno* 92a–95a; *Alcibiades I* 118b–19b, 124c–d.

4. I do not mean to suggest that because Aristophanes and Plato point to these dangers that they were entirely opposed to the use of rhetoric. A more nuanced assessment of the status of rhetoric is suggested by Aristophanes' own use of comic poetry and by Socrates' demonstration of rhetorical speech making in the last section of the *Gorgias*.

5. See Larry Arnhart, *Aristotle on Political Reasoning* (DeKalb: Northern Illinois University Press, 1981); Carnes Lord, "The Intention of Aristotle's *Rhetoric*," *Hermes: Zeitschrift fur classische Philologie* 109 (1981): 326–39; and Mary Nichols, "Aristotle's Defense of Rhetoric," *Journal of Politics* 49 (1987): 657–77.

6. Arnhart, *Political Reasoning*, esp. pp. 24–32; cf. Nichols, "Defense of Rhetoric," esp. pp. 667–69.

7. Aristotle's moral-political writings provide ample evidence of the kind of truths to be extracted from common opinion. See, for example, *NE* 1.8.1098b9–99b8; 9.8.1168a28–69b2; *Pol.* 3.13.1283a29–42; 7.2–3.1324a5–25b31.

## CHAPTER 1. THE AUDIENCE OF THE *ETHICS*

1. The most influential are J. L. Ackrill, "Aristotle on *Eudaimonia*," in *Essays on Aristotle's Ethics*, ed. A. Rorty (Berkeley: University of Califonia Press, 1980), pp. 15–33; and John Cooper, *Reason and Human Good in Aristotle* (Cambridge: Harvard University Press, 1975; rpt. Indianapolis: Hackett Publishing Company, 1986). Cf. Thomas Nagel, "Aristotle on *Eudaimonia*," *Phronesis* 17 (1972): 252–259; Martha Nussbaum, *The Fragility of Goodness* (Cambridge: Cambridge University Press, 1986), esp. pp. 373–377; Georges Rodier, *Études de Philosophie Grecque* (Paris: Librairie Philosophique J. Vrin, 1957); and Kathleen Wilkes, "The Good Man and the Good for Man in Aristotle's Ethics," *Mind* 87 (1978): 553–571.

2. This includes, among others, Stephen Clark, *Aristotle's Man: Speculations upon Aristotelian Anthropology* (Oxford: Clarendon Press, 1975); W. F. R. Hardie, "The Final Good in Aristotle's *Ethics*," *Philosophy* 40 (1965): 277–95; idem, *Aristotle's Ethical Theory* (Oxford: Clarendon Press, 1968), esp. pp. 12–27; idem, "Aristotle on the Best Life for a Man," *Philosophy* 54 (1979): 35–50; David Keyt, "Intellectualism in Aristotle," in *Essays in Ancient Greek Philosophy*, eds. Anton and Preus, vol. 2 (Albany: State University of New York Press, 1984), pp. 364–387; Richard Kraut, *Aristotle on the Human Good* (Princeton, N.J.: Princeton University Press, 1989); Carnes Lord, *Education and Culture in the Political Thought of Aristotle* (Ithaca, N.Y.: Cornell University, 1982); and Amélie Oksenberg Rorty, "The Place of Contemplation in Aristotle's *Nicomachean Ethics*," in *Essays on Aristotle's Ethics*, ed. A. Rorty (Berkeley: University of California Press, 1980), pp. 377–394. Taking his bearings from the *Metaphysics*, Gerald Mara argues for a nuanced compatibility between philosophy and politics (and, by extension, ethics) in Aristotle. See his "The Role of Philosophy in Aristotle's Political Science," *Polity* 19 (Spring 1987): 375–401.

3. The delineation of two major lines of interpretation does not mean that all those who advocate one approach agree with each other about the particular issues or even general conclusions involved in that line of interpretation.

4. For this synopsis of Ackrill's position, see "Aristotle on *Eudaimonia*," esp. pp. 28–33.

5. This summary is drawn from Cooper's *Reason and Human Good*, esp. pp. 151, 167, and 176. Cooper's influential diagnosis of the problem is illuminating despite the subsequent modification of his position in "Contemplation and Happiness: A Reconsideration," in *Moral Philosophy: Historical and Contemporary Essays*, eds. William Starr and Richard Taylor (Milwaukee: Marquette University Press, 1989). Cooper eventually revises his conclusion because he is reluctant to accept the apparent inconsistency that he believes

must be attributed to Aristotle as a consequence of his adoption of an "intellectualist ideal" in Book X.

6. The following summary of Hardie's position is taken from "Aristotle on the Best Life," esp. pp. 35, 42, 46 and *Ethical Theory*, esp. pp. 22–23.

7. This paragraph provides a brief summary of *Aristotle on the Human Good.* For a critical appreciation of Kraut's book as a whole, see Aristide Tessitore's review in *Interpretation* 19 (Spring 1992): 315–18.

8. Leo Strauss, *Natural Right and History* (Chicago: Chicago University Press, 1953); idem, *The City and Man* (Chicago: Chicago University Press, 1964; rpt. Midway, 1977); and Harry Jaffa, *Aristotelianism and Thomism: A Study of the Commentary by Thomas Aquinas on the* Nicomachean Ethics (Chicago: Chicago University Press, 1952; rpt. Greenwood Press, 1979).

9. Strauss, *City and Man*, esp. pp. 21–28.

10. About Jaffa's book, Alasdair MacIntyre writes that "it is an unduly neglected minor classic." *After Virtue* (Notre Dame: University of Notre Dame Press, [1981] 1984), p. 278. Cf. Hardie, "Magnanimity in Aristotle's *Ethics*," *Phronesis* 23 (1978): 63–79, p. 77, n. 7. It should be noted that Strauss's comments are directed more generally to Aristotle's political works as a whole and that Jaffa's study of Aristotle and Aquinas does not include any explicit or thematic consideration of the intended audience of the *Ethics*.

11. See Lord's introduction to *Essays on the Foundations of Aristotelian Political Science*, eds. Carnes Lord and David K. O'Connor (Berkeley: University of California Press, 1991), pp. 1–10 and Lord's *Education and Culture*, pp. 30–33.

12. The following paragraph summarizes Bodéüs's argument in *The Political Dimensions of Aristotle's Ethics*, trans. by Jan Edward Garrett (Albany: State University of New York Press, 1993). See esp. pp. 60–61 and ch. 4.

13. There is, of course, a scholarly tradition that denies any structural unity to the *Ethics* as a whole, viewing it as a somewhat random compilation of lecture notes. Against this view, A. Rorty provides a useful and sensible starting point. She writes, "Even if the book is a thing composed of threads and patches, the organization of those threads and patches composes a perfectly coherent pattern." *Essays on Aristotle's Ethics*, ed. A. Rorty (Berkeley: University of California Press, 1980), p. 3.

14. As this argument suggests, Aristotle's criticism of young students of ethics does not necessarily refer to the chronologically young but rather the immature (1095a6–11).

15. Aristotle qualifies his initial statements about *orthos logos* in Book VI where the expression is identified with prudence. Nevertheless, as we shall have

occasion to see in chapter 2, even Aristotle's fuller account of *orthos logos* in Book VI presupposes some vision of the good as it appears to decent human beings.

16. Given the awkward and dated connotations of the English "gentleman," I have retained the original Greek wherever possible. Aristotle's most thematic discussion of *kalokagathia* is found at *Eudemian Ethics* 1248b8–1249a18. For analyses of the meaning of the term in classical literature, see G. E. M. Ste. De Croix, *The Origins of the Peloponnesian War* (London: Duckworth, 1972), pp. 371–76; K. J. Dover, *Greek Popular Morality in the Time of Plato and Aristotle* (Berkeley: University of California Press, 1974; rpt. Hackett Inc., 1994), pp. 41–45; Leo Strauss, *Natural Right and History*, pp. 142–43; and idem, *City and Man*, pp. 21, 25–28. Cf. Lord, *Education and Culture*, p. 32; Josiah Ober, *Mass and Elite in Democratic Athens: Rhetoric, Ideology, and the Power of the People* (Princeton, N.J.: Princeton University Press, 1989), pp. 251–261; and J. O. Urmson, *Aristotle's Ethics* (Oxford: Basil Blackwell, 1988), p. 3.

17. With respect to the need for economic well-being, see *Pol.* 4.8. 1293b34–42, 4.8.1294a17–19; cf. *NE* 10.8.1178a23–78b3.

18. Although each expression carries its own shade of meaning, Aristotle often uses *spoudaios*, *epieikēs*, and their cognates interchangeably (see, e.g., 10.6.1176b23–27; 10.5.1175b24–28; 9.8.1169a16–20). An initial reference to the morally serious person in the *Nicomachean Ethics* explains that such an individual is characterized by fine judgment about "good and noble things" (*agathai to kai kalai*), that is, the specific attributes of the *kalos k'agathos* (1.8.1099a22–23).

19. Josiah Ober provides an excellent sociopolitical analysis of this phenomenon in *Mass and Elite in Democratic Athens*. See esp. pp. 11–17; 208–212. Stephen Salkever argues persuasively that Aristotle is sharply critical of the code of the gentleman as it was actually lived in the ancient polis. See his "Women, Soldiers, Citizens: Plato and Aristotle on the Politics of Virility," in *Essays on the Foundations of Aristotelian Political Science*, eds. Lord and O'Connor (Berkeley: University of California Press, 1991), pp. 165–190.

20. In the *Rhetoric* (2.15–16.1390b14–91a19) Aristotle is harshly critical of many who belong to the social-political class of notables. Those who enjoy the advantages of good birth or wealth are characterized as "worthless" (*euteles*) or "foolish" (*aonoetos*). The powerful fare only slightly better. They are said to be more "honor-loving" (*philotimoteroi*) and "manly" (*andrōdesteroi*) than the rich (1391a20–b4), but both of these attributes are given, at best, an ambiguous place in Aristotle's political analysis. See Salkever, "Politics of Virility."

21. Marilyn B. Arthur gives expression to what may be a more pervasive view when she writes that "the philosophy of Aristotle, unlike that of Plato, is

a codification of general social practice, a systematization of social values."
"Review Essay: Classics," *Signs* 2 (1976): 382–404, p. 394; cf. Hannah Arendt,
*The Human Condition* (Chicago: Chicago University Press, 1958), p. 27; and A.
MacIntyre, *A Short History of Ethics* (New York: Macmillan Inc., 1966), pp. 67–
68. Against this view, Jonathan Barnes maintains that Aristotle's method of
studying ethics does not commit him to the "conservative parochialism" of
common practice. See his "Aristotle and the Methods of Ethics," *Revue Internationale de Philosophie* 34 (1980): 490–511.

22. The degree to which Aristotle succeeds in transcending his own cul-
tural matrix is in some measure suggested by what can only be described as a
contemporary renaissance of Aristotelian studies in ethics and politics. MacIntyre's *After Virtue* and James Q. Wilson's *The Moral Sense* (New York: Macmillan Inc., 1993) are indicative of the scope of Aristotle's continued influence
in moral philosophy and social science. Although I do not simply endorse his
categories, John Wallach attests to the rich variety of Aristotelian perspectives
that continue to gain momentum in a number of contemporary moral-political debates. See Wallach's "Contemporary Aristotelianism," *Political Theory* 20
(November 1992): 613–641.

23. Callicles, in a harsh but revealing way, gives expression to precisely
this antagonism between the life of the philosopher and that of the *kalos k'agathos* (*Gorgias* 484c–e; cf. *Meno* 92e–95a).

24. Mary Nichols contends that Aristotle's political philosophy should
itself be viewed as an act of statesmanship. See Nichols, *Citizens and Statesmen:
A Study of Aristotle's Politics* (Savage, Maryland: Rowman & Littlefield, 1992),
pp. 7–9.

25. This is the locus of my disagreement with Ackrill who maintains that
Aristotle is advocating an inclusive theory of happiness at this point in the
argument.

26. The susceptibility of human happiness to the vagaries of "luck" is an
important Aristotelian theme ably developed by Martha Nussbaum in *The
Fragility of Goodness*, esp. chs. 11–12. Cf. Bernard Yack, *The Problems of a Political Animal: Community, Justice, and Conflict in Aristotelian Political Thought*
(Los Angeles: University of California Press, 1993), esp. ch. 8.

27. Although agreeing with Hardie on the open-ended character of the
argument in Book I, I agree with Ackrill that the thrust of Aristotle's argument
in this book supports an "inclusive" understanding of the human good. I differ
from Ackrill in that I attribute this understanding of the argument to the
reader and do not identify it with Aristotle's own position. Aristotle's argument in Book I is characterized by an irreducible ambiguity; the attempt to dis-

pel that ambiguity, however appealing, necessarily introduces greater precision than Aristotle considers appropriate at this point in his study.

28. This is, in fact, a debated question. In *Aristotle's First Principles*
(Oxford: Oxford University, 1988), Terence Irwin maintains that Aristotle's
moral and political teachings rest upon metaphysical and psychological principles. Salkever makes a similar argument with respect to Aristotle's biology,
which he considers essential to a proper understanding of his political thought.
See Salkever, "Politics of Virility," p. 172. Strauss maintains that Aristotle,
unlike Plato, succeeded in founding political science as a practical discipline in
a way that does not make it dependent upon theoretical science. See Strauss,
*City and Man*, pp. 21–28.

## CHAPTER 2. THE VIRTUES

1. Aristotle had actually introduced this second kind of consideration
toward the end of Book I where he offered an initial argument for the view that
a life characterized by the practice of virtue is also a pleasant life (1.8.1099a7–
21).

2. This second or intermediate treatment of pleasure is, in fact, the dominant one in the *Ethics*. As we shall see, it is given its fullest expression in Book
X, when Aristotle returns in a thematic way to the issue of happiness that provided the occasion for his initial cursory treatment of pleasure in Book I.

3. This problem will receive a fuller treatment in Aristotle's discussion of
intellectual virtue in Book VI.

4. Robert Faulkner observes that this account is "the most optimistic as to
human power in the whole *Ethics*." He goes on to note that the emphasis on
human power and responsibility is "somehow extreme" and eventually qualified. "Spontaneity, Justice, and Coercion: On *Nicomachean Ethics* Books III
and V," in *Nomos*, vol. 14, *Coercion*, eds. J. Roland Pennock and John W.
Chapman (Chicago: Aldine/Atherton Press, 1972), pp. 81–106, see esp. pp.
101–02.

5. Aristotle's awareness of the problematic character of this argument is
suggested in the following way. He points out that character is not voluntary
in the same way that action is (3.5.1114b30–15a3). Whereas we are in control
of action from beginning to end (when we know the particulars), we are in
control of character only at the beginning since each separate choice has an
imperceptible effect in shaping character in a way that reduces its susceptibility
to human agency. Aristotle has, however, already indicated that the kind of
habits we are trained in from childhood is all important (2.1.1103b23–25).

Putting these assertions together suggests that we may not be responsible in the crucial case for those habits from which our character originates, but that this results from a certain kind of education or upbringing.

6. For an enlightening account of the pivotal, if subterranean, role of *nemesis* in the *Ethics*, see Ronna Burger, "Ethical Reflection and Righteous Indignation : Nemesis in the *Nicomachean Ethics*," in *Essays in Ancient Greek Philosophy*, eds. John P. Anton and Anthony Preus, vol. 4, *Aristotle's Ethics* (Albany: State University of New York Press, 1991), pp. 127–39.

7. Hardie reports the bewildering array of scholarly interpretations in "Magnanimity in Aristotle's Ethics," *Phronesis* 23 (1978): 63–79. Several observations in the following discussion are indebted to Hardie's excellent discussion.

8. Hardie points out that in the first thirty lines, "greatness" (*megethos*) and "worth" (*axia*) with their variants occur on almost every line. Ibid., p. 73.

9. This is not to deny that magnanimous persons "think slightly of" (*kataphroneō*) those who do not take their bearings from *kalokagathia* (4.3.1124b5–6), although their use of irony in speaking with those who fall below them may in some measure conceal this fact (4.3.1124b29–31).

10. Aquinas labors mightily to provide plausible explanations for these seemingly insignificant details. He strains even more in seeking to make magnanimity compatible with biblical humility. See *Summa Theologiae* II-II, qu. 129 and qu. 161. For a discussion of Aquinas's insightful but problematic interpretation of magnanimity, see Jaffa, *Thomism and Aristotelianism*, esp. pp. 134–41.

11. This discussion of Aristotle's reference to magnanimity in the *Posterior Analytics* is indebted to Réné Gauthier, *Magnanimité: L'Idéal de la Grandeur dans la Philosophie Païenne et dans la Théologie Chrétienne* (Paris: Librairie Philosophique J. Vrin, 1951), esp. pp. 17–40.

12. Ibid., p. 116.

13. Hardie, "Magnanimity," esp. pp. 70–73.

14. Larry Arnhart, "Statesmanship as Magnanimity: Classical, Christian and Modern," *Polity* 16 (Winter 1983): 263–83, p. 267.

15. The case of Socrates is obviously different; it would be hard to construe him as a *kalos k'agathos* by any standard. Still, even in this case, Aristotle attempts to soften the conflict between philosophy and politics for which Socrates' life and death became emblematic. For a discussion of this point, see Aristide Tessitore, "Aristotle's Political Presentation of Socrates in the *Nicomachean Ethics*," *Interpretation* 16 (Fall 1988): 3–22.

16. Consider Aristotle's later statements at 10.8.1178b3–5 and 1179a3–9.

17. The awkward but more conventional terminology for justice in the first sense is "universal justice." This translation is misleading in the measure that it connotes quantitative rather than qualitative characteristics that are both worldwide and absolute. Aristotle actually describes the first meaning of justice with reference to perfect or complete virtue (*teleia aretē*) (5.1.1129b26) and identifies it with the whole of virtue (*holē aretē*) because it includes all the other virtues (5.1.1130a8–9). It is this meaning of justice that I have translated as "comprehensive justice."

18. The various meanings of justice distinguished by Aristotle in Book V (comprehensive or universal, particular, political, conventional, natural, distributive, corrective, reciprocal, and equitable) as he, to some extent, acknowledges (5.1.1129a26–29), are notoriously difficult to systematize and have given rise to a variety of different classifications. Justifications for the particular distinctions and relations that frame the following discussion are offered in the body of the text. In particular, I do not find sufficient textual support in the *Nicomachean Ethics* for the influential but essentially scholastic conception of a divine or unwritten law (universal and unchanging) that is able to furnish an independent and salutary standard for the particular and varying laws encountered in actual political practice.

19. David K. O'Connor provides an excellent account of Aristotle's distinction between simple and relational virtue. The former "aetiological" perspective focuses on a person's psychic state; the latter "symptomological" one concerns the political manifestations of virtue and vice. See O'Connor, "The Aetiology of Justice," in *Essays on the Foundations of Political Science*, eds. Lord and O'Connor (Berkeley: University of California Press, 1991), pp. 136–164.

20. O'Connor maintains that Aristotle's account of relational virtue is distinct from but not in conflict with his account of simple virtue. I think this is only partially correct. O'Connor's clarification successfully dissipates apparent inconsistencies in Aristotle's treatment that arise from a failure to recognize the different perspectives that distinguish his account of justice from his consideration of the other ethical virtues. However, Aristotle does not dissolve the conflict intrinsic to ethical virtue itself. This becomes most apparent by considering ethical virtue at its peak. O'Connor glosses over this problem at least in part because he defines magnanimity in relation to honor, an external good that is also one of the objects of justice, rather than by its relation to the noble, a concern that virtually disappears in the consideration of justice. This problem is treated more fully below.

21. Although the case of distributive justice is somewhat more ambiguous, Aristotle clearly emphasizes its relation to equality in the *Ethics*. Cf.

5.3.1131a10–24 and 1131a24–32. The emphasis on equality that underlies Aristotle's discussion of the various species of particular justice also appears to constitute the specific character of political justice in contradistinction to "the simply just." See 5.6.1134a24–30.

22. Consider Aristotle's qualified endorsement of the justice of ostracism at *Politics* 3.13.1284b15–20.

23. What is presupposed is the kind of character that leads one to prefer doing justice to injustice. The absence of any reference to *hexis* in the body of the discussion is consistent with the preoccupation with external actions characteristic of a civic perspective.

24. In reflecting on the practical aim of Aristotle's study of ethics, Robert Faulkner writes: "Some exaggeration of human powers is salutary. To say that effort doesn't matter deters effort that could matter, and some exaggeration of the power of effort encourages effort." "Spontaneity, Justice, and Coercion," p. 87.

25. I am reluctant to translate *politikē* as political science since it also refers to political art or skill. It is certainly misleading to think of *politikē* as science in the strict sense since it is part of the unscientific *phronēsis*. I have translated *politikē* as political capacity since this preserves better the various connotations consistent with Aristotelian usage.

26. This distinction parallels that between comprehensive and particular justice. Cf. 6.8.1141b23–24 and 5.1.1130a12–13.

27. Notwithstanding the many merits of C. D. C. Reeve's incisive study, he is mistaken in removing prudence from the sphere of politics. See Reeve, *Practices of Reason: Aristotle's Nicomachean Ethics* (Oxford: Clarendon Press, 1992), esp. p. 76.

28. In the *Politics*, Aristotle says that prudence is the only virtue peculiar to the ruler (3.4.1277b25–26).

29. Aristotle makes the connection between prudence and equity explicit at 6.11.1143a25–35.

30. We have reached the penultimate stage in Aristotle's argument about the architectonic character of politics. The claim that politics is the most architectonic discipline originally advanced in Book I reached its high point in Aristotle's discussion of comprehensive justice (V.1). This view was qualified by his discussion of equity (V.10) and now more definitively by his statement about legislative capacity (VI.8), both of which characterize the individual of practical wisdom. The final stage of the argument is not reached until Book VII when Aristotle reveals that it is the political philosopher who is architect of the end at which politics aims (VII.11.1152b1–3).

31. Thucydides reports that under the leadership of Pericles, Athens was a democracy in name but was in fact ruled by its first citizen. *Histories* 2.65.9–10. Cf. Plutarch's "Pericles," esp. 9,11,15.

32. This does not necessarily imply that prudence deliberates about means and not ends. Several scholars have successfully challenged this narrow conception of prudence. See David Wiggins, "Deliberation and Practical Reason," in *Essays on Aristotle's Ethics*, ed. A. Rorty (Berkeley: University of California Press, 1980), pp. 221–240; and Richard Sorabji, "Aristotle on the Role of Intellect in Virtue," in *Essays on Aristotle's Ethics*, ed. A. Rorty (Berkeley: University of California Press, 1980), pp. 201–219. Nevertheless, a question remains as to whether the first principles of prudence derive from philosophic scrutiny or uninstructed experience. Aristotle emphasizes the latter as a practical matter (6.8.1142a11–23; 6.11.1143b6–17) but does not altogether rule out the former (7.11.1152b1–3).

33. Aristotle's argument refers specifically to *nous* (6.13.1144b9,12), a term he uses in different ways. *Nous* sometimes refers to the rational part of the soul as a whole (6.2.1139a17–18, 33–34), a usage that encompasses both practical and theoretical intelligence. It also possesses a restricted and particular meaning as that part of the theoretical intelligence that apprehends undemonstrable first principles (1140b31–41a8). In the present context, *nous* is used to describe something that falls within the broader sphere of *phronēsis*.

34. Georges Rodier expresses the problematic character of Aristotle's exposition when he writes, "Il faut, en un sens, être déjà vertueux pour le devenir." *Études de Philosophie Grecque* (Paris: Librarie Philosophique J. Vrin, 1957), p. 184. Aristotle's cryptic explanation of the role of *nous* in practical reasoning (6.11.1143a35–43b5) recasts rather than resolves the circular character of this argument. Perception of the first principles of ethics proves to be the result of a process of habituation among those fortunate enough to enjoy a decent upbringing. For an excellent discussion of this point, see Reeve, *Practices of Reason*, esp. pp. 56–66; 84–87.

35. A sense of the magnitude of Aristotle's restraint in bringing these limitations to light becomes evident when it is compared to Nietzsche's harsher articulation of the same problem. About Socrates, Nietzsche writes: "What did he do his life long but laugh at the awkward incapacity of noble Athenians, who, like all noble men, were men of instinct and never could give sufficient information about the reasons for their action?" *Beyond Good and Evil*, 191.

36. Reeve argues that the wisdom in question is "first philosophy" or "theology" in his *Practices of Reason*, esp. ch. 4, pp. 139–45. Cf. Pierre Defourny, "Contemplation in Aristotle's Ethics," in *Articles on Aristotle*, eds. Barnes, Schofield and Sorabji, vol. 2, *Ethics and Politics* (New York: St. Martin's

Press, 1978), pp. 104–113. Although I believe this is correct, it is nevertheless a source of puzzlement that Aristotle should choose such bland examples (white, straight, and the beings from which the cosmos is composed) to introduce his distinction between the most exalted activity of wisdom and the lower activities of prudence and politics (6.7.1141a20–41b3).

37. Aristotle's characterization of Thales and Anaxagoras does not seem quite fair. Among other things, Thales was well known for successfully monopolizing the olive press market as well as attempting to organize a Hellenic confederation to counter the Persian threat. Anaxagoras was the personal advisor of Pericles and deeply, if indirectly, involved in Athenian politics. As I suggest in the sequel, Aristotle's extreme characterization of Thales and Anaxagoras may be part of an ironic commentary on the absence of any political philosophy in their theoretical investigations of nature. Viewed in this light, the actual and conspicuous involvement of Thales and Anaxagoras in practical affairs may point to a certain inadequacy or incompleteness in their philosophic teachings; both failed to give sufficient theoretical weight to the distinctive and pivotal character of human nature in the attempt to provide an intelligible account of nature as a whole.

38. Book VI begins and ends with images drawn from medicine; indeed, such images recur as a leitmotif throughout this book (6.1.1138b30–32; 6.5.1140a27; 6.7.1141a31–33; 6.7.1141b18–21; 6.10.1143a3; 6.12.1143b25–28; 6.12.1144a3–6; 6.13.1145a6–9). Werner Jaeger maintains that, far from being a casual analogy, Aristotle's references to medicine belong to the very foundation of his ethical science in general, and his distinction between prudence and wisdom in particular. See Jaeger, "Aristotle's Use of Medicine as Model of Method in his Ethics," *Journal of Hellenic Studies* 77–78 (1957–58): pp. 54–61. See esp. pp. 57, 59.

39. This argument is, as we shall see, qualified but not retracted in Aristotle's thematic consideration of happiness in Book X.

## CHAPTER 3. A NEW BEGINNING

1. There is no suitable English translation for *akrasia* and *enkrateia*. I retain the traditional *incontinence* and *continence* simply because none of the alternatives seem better. On the inadequacy of English translations of *akrasia* and *enkrateia*, see A. Rorty, "Akrasia and Pleasure," in *Essays on Aristotle's Ethics*, ed. A. Rorty (Berkeley: University of California Press, 1980), pp. 267–84, p. 283, n. 1. For a discussion of the precise meaning and philosophic background against which these terms are used by Aristotle, see *L'Éthique à Nicomaque*, eds. Réné Gauthier and Jean Jolif, vol. 2 (Louvain: Publications Universitaires, 1970), pp. 579–581.

2. Aristotle refers to a godlike excellence more honorable than virtue (*hē timiōteron aretēs*) (7.1.1145a26), a phrase that recalls his earlier definition of wisdom as a science of the most honorable things (*epistēmē tōn timiōtatōn*) (6.7.1141a18–20). As we saw in the preceding chapter, the broader scope of wisdom reveals the comparatively narrow focus of politics and prudence, and at least partially accounts for the greater seriousness (*spoudaiotatē*) (6.7.1141a20–41b3) and authority (*kuria*) of the latter (6.13.1145a6–11).

3. This leads Gauthier and Jolif to dismiss Aristotle's reference to heroic virtue as merely dialectical while expressing regret that it does not figure more prominently in his treatise. See *L'Éthique*, vol. 2, pp. 583–585. Hardie, on the other hand, maintains that an account of Aristotle's doctrine of virtue that fails to include "heroic virtue" is incomplete. Hardie's brief appendix is, however, more helpful in calling attention to the need for some positive account of heroic virtue than it is in providing one. See Hardie, "Aristotle's Doctrine that Virtue is a Mean," in *Articles on Aristotle*, eds. Barnes, Schofield, and Sorabji, vol. 2, *Ethics and Politics* (New York: St. Martin's Press, 1978), esp. pp. 42–46.

4. I follow Irwin in translating *aporia* as "puzzle," although I use the alternative translations of "problem" and "difficulty" as well. *Aporia* can also be translated as "dilemma" or "antinomy" and is likened by Aristotle to a knot or tangle (*desmos*) that binds the intelligence (*Meta.* 3.1.995a24–95b5.; cf. *NE* 7.2.1146a21–27). For a discussion of the meaning of *aporia*, see H. H. Joachim, *Aristotle: The Nicomachean Ethics*, ed. D. A. Raes (London: Clarendon Press, 1951), p. 219 and *The Ethics of Aristotle*, ed. John Burnet (London: Methuen, 1900), pp. xl-xli.

5. Burnet incisively points out that it is as if Aristotle says, "We have first to deal with the great *aporia, poteron eidotes ē ou*; and then we can take all the rest together." *Ethics*, p. 298. On the central importance of this first *aporia*, see Hardie, *Ethical Theory*, p. 259.

6. For this rendering of the opening line of the first *aporia* and its interpretative significance, see Hardie, *Ethical Theory*, esp. pp. 262–268.

7. The radical character of Socrates' denial of incontinence becomes most evident when one considers his explanation of what actually occurs. Socrates' analysis of incontinence leads him to assert that there is no good apart from pleasure and that virtue consists in knowing how to choose the greatest pleasure. See *Protag.* 351c–61c, esp. 375a and 358b. Although it is important to take into consideration the rhetorical context within which Socrates makes these claims, it is also true that the harsh character of his investigation is antagonistic to the sensibilities of most decent persons. Although regrettable, it is not surprising that Socrates' mode of inquiry eventually elicited the condemnation of his fellow citizens.

8. The Greek term *phainomena* encompasses both empirical facts and accepted opinions. G. E. L. Owen points out that, in the present context, Socrates' claim conflicts not with the facts but with what is commonly said about them. See Owen, "Tithenai ta Phainomena," in *Aristotle: A Collection of Critical Essays*, ed. J. M. E. Moravcsik (Garden City: Doubleday & Company, Inc., 1967), pp. 167–190, p. 168.

9. For a good account of the range and complexity of the issues involved in this section, see Hardie, *Ethical Theory*, ch. 13, esp. pp. 262–292.

10. Despite widespread agreement about Aristotle's use of these two types of arguments in the present context, there is a remarkable degree of difference in the way these arguments are evaluated. Robert Robinson maintains that the *phusikōs* explanation, although it is often used by Aristotle to present a topic from a distinct and "better" point of view, has in this case no real bearing on what Aristotle takes to be a logical puzzle. See Robinson, "Aristotle on Akrasia," in *Articles on Aristotle*, eds. Barnes, Schofield, and Sorabji, vol. 2, *Ethics and Politics* (New York: St. Martin's Press, 1978), pp. 84–87. Burnet asserts that the first three arguments are essentially dialectical whereas the *phusikōs* explanation reveals Aristotle's real answer to the problem in his *Ethics*, p. 299. James Walsh declares that grouping these four arguments together indicates the absence of any fundamental difference between the two approaches. See Walsh, *Aristotle's Conception of Moral Weakness* (New York: Columbia University Press, 1963), pp. 99–100. John Randall makes the general suggestion that Aristotle normally follows a pattern of investigation that moves from *logikōs* to *phusikōs* as the inquiry is brought into the wider context of nature. See Randall, *Aristotle* (New York: Columbia University Press, 1960), pp. 59–61. I have found Randall's general observation to be borne out in the present case.

11. Owen demonstrates the fluidity of these distinctions, especially as they pertain to the *Physics*. See "Tithenai to Phainomena," esp. pp. 188–190.

12. A. Rorty points out that *pathos* can but need not be passionate. To be moved by *pathos* is "to be moved by something primarily outside oneself, to react rather than act." "Akrasia and Pleasure," p. 275. As we shall see, the behavior of incontinent persons is determined by the nature of their reactions to pleasure.

13. This view runs counter to a scholarly tradition that denies any essential connection between Aristotle's treatments of incontinence and pleasure in Book VII. See, e.g., Gauthier and Jolif, *L'Éthique*, vol. 2, p. 782.

14. This suggestion is made by A. Rorty in "Akrasia and Pleasure," p. 278.

15. It is difficult to find an adequate translation for *melancholikos* because the range of meaning associated with Aristotle's use of the word is limited by

the contemporary meaning of melancholy. In *Problem XXX*, the author indicates that the *melancholikos* possesses a variable temperament that can take a variety of different forms in different people. These include, among others: (1) those who are sluggish and stupid, (2) those who are clever, erotic, easily moved by spiritedness and desire, and some who become talkative, and (3) those touched by madness. All such persons are "extraordinary" (*perissos*), not on account of disease, but by nature.

16. Although the *Problems* are generally considered to be a gradual compilation by different authors within the Peripatetic tradition, they are nevertheless thought to contain authentic Aristotelian passages. The particular discussion referred to here (Book XXX) is cited as genuinely Aristotelian by Cicero and Plutarch.

17. In *Problem XXX* the author provides natural, primarily physiological, explanations to account for the disposition of the *melancholikos* (esp. 955a39–40). At no point in this discussion is the *melancholikos* evaluated from an ethical point of view.

18. A. J. Festugière, *Aristotle: Le Plaisir* (Paris: Librairie Philosophique, 1936; rpt. 1960), pp. xxiv, xxv–xliv. Festugière's interpretation of Aristotle's double account of pleasure as a reflection of different stages in his intellectual development is a particular application of the general thesis pioneered by Werner Jaeger in *Aristotle: Fundamentals of His Development*, trans. by Richard Robinson (Oxford: Clarendon Press, 1948). The problematic character of Jaeger's thesis is incisively stated by Ernest Barker in *The Politics of Aristotle* (London: Oxford University Press, 1946, rpt. 1973), p. xlii.

19. See, for example, Godo Lieberg, *Die Lehre von der Lust in den Ethiken des Aristoteles* (München: C. H. Beck'she, 1958), pp. 2–15; Gauthier and Jolif, *L'Éthique*, vol. 2, p. 783; and F. Dirlmeier, *Aristoteles: Nikomachische Ethik* (Berlin: Akademie Verlag, 1956; rpt. 1979), pp. 567, 580–581. Hardie is more circumspect about the exact relationship between Aristotle's two accounts of pleasure in *Ethical Theory*, p. 295.

20. G. E. L. Owen, "Aristotelian Pleasures," in *Articles on Aristotle*, eds. Barnes, Schofield, and Sorabji, vol. 2, *Ethics and Politics* (New York: St. Martin's Press, 1978), pp. 92–103.

21. About Book X, Owen writes that Aristotle "is offering to tell us what the nature of enjoying is by reviewing the logical characteristics of pleasure verbs." "Pleasures," p. 103. Owen's interpretation abstracts from both the immediate context and overall aim of Aristotle's two treatments of pleasure. As such, he provides a helpful but, for this reason, limited logical-linguistic analysis of the text.

22. Owen, "Pleasures," p. 93. Although Owen's thesis has met with only limited success in displacing the understanding of the problem advanced by Festugière, it has the merit of pointing to the fact that Aristotle's account in Book VII contains a consistent and positive teaching of its own. Further, it leads Owen, and invites his readers, to grapple with the fundamental differences that distinguish this account from the one that appears in Book X.

23. The discomfort provoked by this Aristotelian statement is reflected in the efforts of some scholars to reinterpret its meaning. See, for example, H. H. Joachim, *Aristotle: The Nicomachean Ethics*, ed. D. A. Raes (London: Clarendon Press, 1951), p. 234. Hardie speaks of "political science" rather than political philosophers, something that enables him to harmonize the prologue in Book VII with the more explicitly political prologue of Book X. See Hardie, *Ethical Theory*, p. 299.

24. Gauthier and Jolif, *L'Éthique*, vol. 2, pp. 797–798.

25. The open-ended character of this argument (the activity of all of them [*hexeis*] or the one that constitutes happiness) anticipates the two different views of happiness that Aristotle ranks in Book X: secondary happiness, understood as the unimpeded activity of ethical virtue, and complete or perfect happiness, understood as the more perfectly unimpeded activity of contemplation.

26. The disconcerting character of Aristotle's arguments in Book VII did not escape his earliest commentators. As Gauthier and Jolif point out, it was precisely in order to avoid the "disastrous consequence" of a teaching identifying pleasure with happiness that Aspasius, Alexander of Aphrodisias, and Nemesius insisted on the importance of Aristotle's "correction" of this teaching in Book X. See *L'Éthique*, vol. 2, pp. 780–781. The seriousness of Aristotle's defense of hedonism has been argued by H. A. Prichard in "The Meaning of *Agathon* in the *Ethics* of Aristotle," in *Aristotle: A Collection of Critical Essays*, ed. Moravsik (Garden City: Doubleday & Company, Inc., 1967), pp. 241–260.

27. As we saw in chapter 1, Aristotle's initial and open-ended conclusion in Book I identified happiness with the activity of "complete virtue" *or*, should there prove to be several, "the one that is best and most complete" (1.7.1098a16–18). The same ambiguity is retained in his initial clarifications of the relationship between virtue and pleasure (1.8.1099a29–31) and virtue and fortune (1.10.1101a14–15). Aristotle neither specifies the substantive content of "complete virtue" nor makes explicit the exact relationship of theoretical and ethical virtue to happiness at this point in his study.

28. As we shall see, Aristotle offers very different kinds of arguments when he returns to this issue in Book X.

29. Thomas Nagel captures the harsh character of this teaching when he writes, "[T]his is essentially a caretaker function of reason, in which it is occupied with matters . . . far below those that it might be considering if it had more time and were less called upon merely to *manage.*" "Aristotle on *Eudaimonia,*" in *Essays on Aristotle's Ethics*, ed. A. Rorty (Berkeley: University of California Press, 1980), p. 12. It is important to add, however, that this view of ethical virtue is, at most, implicit in Books I–VI, comes to light most clearly in Book VII, and is qualified but not retracted in Book X.

## CHAPTER 4. VIRTUE, FRIENDSHIP, AND PHILOSOPHY

1. Aristotle subsequently reduces the ground of friendship to goodness or pleasure since it is possible to understand usefulness in these terms (8.2. 1155b19–21).

2. Michael Pakaluk maintains that there is no overarching genus for the three kinds of friendship. Friendship among the good "stands to the other kinds of friendship as a good in the category of substance stands to a good in the category of accident." "Friendship and the Comparison of Goods," *Phronesis* 37 (1992): 111–130, p. 129. Cf. W. W. Fortenbaugh, "Aristotle's Analysis of Friendship: Function and Analogy, Resemblance, and Focal Meaning," *Phronesis* 20 (1975): 51–62. John Cooper is the leading advocate for the view that there is a more substantial continuity among the three types of friendship. He argues that Aristotle includes a place for disinterestedness even in the inferior types. See Cooper, "Forms of Friendship," *Review of Metaphysics* 30 (1977): 619–48. For a critical assessment of Cooper's position, see Kenneth Alpern, "Aristotle on the Friendships of Utility and Pleasure," *Journal of the History of Philosophy* 21 (1983): 303–315.

3. Kant provides a clear illustration of this situation. He describes a strong and morally upright individual who through suffering or natural disposition is not characterized by a genuine affection for others. One can easily imagine that such persons would have the respect of others but not necessarily their friendship. See *Grounding for a Metaphysics of Morals*, 398–99.

4. Simple equality might be considered a sixth characteristic of friendship. Although it is possible for unequals to be friends, friendship in the fullest and best sense exists between equals.

5. As noted in chapter 2, this same case also poses a special problem for political justice. The best that can be done under these circumstances is to turn over political authority to the individual of surpassing virtue. Although this does not provide a fully adequate solution to the political problem, it is, Aristotle asserts, what justice requires (*Pol.* 3.17.1288a15–29).

6. Although the case of "companions" or "comrades" (*hetairoi*) is ambiguous, in the present context these relationships are reckoned among fraternal friendships (8.12.1162a9–16).

7. Aristotle's assertion about the naturalness of the polis in Book I of the *Politics* is well known. Less well known but equally important, are the several ways in which he qualifies without retracting that claim throughout the rest of his study. For a penetrating discussion of the problem, see Wayne Ambler, "Aristotle's Understanding of the Naturalness of the City," *Review of Politics* 47 (1985): 163–185.

8. Aristotle's references to philosophy in the opening and closing chapters of Book IX are probably not accidental. Toward the beginning of this book, he blithely asserts the incommensurable debt of gratitude owed to those who have shared the activity of philosophy with us (9.1.1164b3–6). Book IX concludes with an understated reference to the possibility of philosophic friendship (9.12.1172a5).

9. In the present context Aristotle uses *dianoia*, *phronēsis*, and *nous* to indicate the rational part of the soul (9.4.1166a13–23). However, he refers specifically to *nous* when he speaks of that which is, or is more than anything else, oneself. As we have had occasion to note, the meaning that Aristotle attaches to *nous* in the *NE* is ambiguous. In IX.4 and 8, *nous* refers predominately to practical intelligence. In X.7, Aristotle gently but clearly shifts that usage from the general to the specific meaning of *nous*, acknowledging but then dropping any reference to practical reason as he focuses more exclusively on the contemplative excellence of theoretical intelligence.

10. Charles Kahn proposes a literal reading of the *allos autos* formula, anticipating Aristotle's later identification of *nous* with our true self in X.7. Kahn argues that since the *nous* of all human beings is fundamentally one and the same, in perfect friendship each person recognizes at least implicitly that the true self of the other is identical with his or her own true self. See Kahn, "Aristotle and Altruism," *Mind* 40 (1981): 20–40, pp. 34–40.

11. Kahn contrasts the relative lack of interest in the concept of self-love in *EE* VII.6 with the account in *NE* IX.4. Whereas the *Eudemian* version derives the possibility of friendship with oneself from the paradigm of friendship among the virtuous, the *Nicomachean* consideration maintains that it is only *because* the good are friends to themselves that they can be friends to one another. See "Aristotle and Altruism," pp. 27–28.

12. Bernard Yack makes the strongest case for the view that political friendship is shared advantage friendship in his provocative and excellent book, *The Problems of a Political Animal*, esp. ch. 4.

13. A. W. Price is also impressed by the need to understand the discussion of political friendship in light of Aristotle's teaching on the aim of the polis, something that leads him to conclude that civic friendship is an extended variant of full virtue friendship. See his *Love and Friendship in Plato and Aristotle* (Oxford: Clarendon Press, 1989), pp. 193–205.

14. Paul Rahe's thorough and illuminating discussions of *homonoia* also reflect the tension between utility and virtue embedded in Aristotle's consideration of political friendship. See Rahe, *Republics Ancient and Modern*, vol. 1, *The Ancien Régime in Classical Greece* (Chapel Hill: University of North Carolina Press, 1994).

15. In the *Eudemian Ethics*, Aristotle distinguishes the primary and natural meaning of *homonoia* among morally serious persons from the weaker and broader consensus about ruling and being ruled that constitutes political friendship (*EE* 7.7.1241a16–33).

16. Elijah Millgram suggests, in large measure because of the argument in this chapter, that in Aristotle's view individuals quite literally "make" their friends. One becomes causally responsible for who one's friend is to the extent that one contributes to the development or exercise of those virtues that lie at the core of his or her identity. See Millgram, "Aristotle on Making Other Selves," *Canadian Journal of Philosophy* 17 (June 1987): 361–376. Nancy Sherman also gives prominence to the way in which friends mold or shape each other. See "Aristotle on Friendship and the Shared Life," *Philosophy and Phenomenological Research* 48 (June 1987): 589–613, pp. 605, 610.

17. The relationship between benefactors and beneficiaries fails to qualify as primary friendship because of the absence of simple equality. Aristotle's argument in this chapter also emphasizes the inability of beneficiaries to "equalize" the relationship by returning a proportionately larger share of affection. He explains that the feeling of friendliness attaches to the more active party who expends greater effort whereas beneficiaries are essentially passive (9.7.1168a19–27).

18. Julia Annas attempts to avoid this conclusion by introducing a distinction between conscious and unconscious motivation: self-love underlies but does not consciously motivate the sacrifices of morally serious persons. See Annas, "Self-Love in Aristotle," *The Southern Journal of Philosophy* 27 (1988): 1–18, esp. pp. 12–13. Cf. Kahn "Aristotle and Altruism," pp. 24–26. Even if Annas correctly describes the mental state of the majority of Aristotle's readers (as I believe she does), there is nothing in Aristotle's argument that excludes greater self-consciousness about one's motivation, especially for those not entirely satisfied with the noble imprecision in self-knowledge implied by Annas's distinction.

## CHAPTER 5. MAKING THE CITY SAFE FOR PHILOSOPHY

1. The exceptions concern two of Eudoxus's arguments in support of the view that pleasure is the good. Eudoxus observes that all things seek pleasure and avoid pain and that pleasure is sought as an end in itself. Although Aristotle's subsequent clarification provides an implicit alternative to these arguments, it should also be recalled that Aristotle had himself employed comparable evidence in defense of the view now attributed to Eudoxus. The fact that all beings seek pleasure was cited by Aristotle to support the view that pleasure is the supreme good (7.13.1153b25–32). Similarly, his argument that some pleasures enjoy the status of ends was intended to demonstrate that there need not be anything better than pleasure (7.12.1153a7–11). The absence of an explicit critique for these two Eudoxian arguments might prompt attentive students to recall Aristotle's earlier endorsement of these positions.

2. Aristotle later uses the same verb (*suzeugnumi*) to describe the relationship between prudence and moral virtue (10.8.1178a16–17). Both the dismissal of the question of pleasure (to which we will return) and subsequent argument about prudence and pleasure share the same degree of clarity as his circular exposition of the relationship between prudence and moral virtue in Book VI. Cf. 6.12.1144a20–31 and 6.13.1144b21–24.

3. As we have had occasion to observe, Aristotle considers a similar problem in Book I; namely, that pleasure, especially sensual pleasure, appears to constitute happiness for human beings. In that context, however, he simply disparages this view, maintaining that such a life is equally well suited to cattle (1.5.1095b14–22; see 2.9.1109b7–12).

4. The morally debilitating effect of the example of the powerful appears to motivate Polus's attack on Socrates in the *Gorgias*. Polus maintains that everyone, including Socrates, consciously or unconsciously envies the powerful (468e; 470e–71e).

5. Aristotle is elsewhere more forthcoming about the difference between the moral-political and contemplative ways of life. One might recall, for example, his differentiation of three ways of life at the outset of the *Ethics* (1.5.1095b14–96a5) or the discussion of prudence and wisdom and the different exemplars supplied for each (see 6.5.1140a24–b11; 6.7.1141a20–b14). His reference in the *Politics* to the dispute between those who agree that the most choiceworthy life is accompanied by virtue explicitly acknowledges the magnitude of the controversy that he plays down in the present context (see, esp. *Pol.* 7.2.1324a25–35).

6. The kinship between excellent practical activity and contemplation is central in Kraut's interpretation of the *Ethics*. See esp. pp. 58–59, 325.

7. I agree with Germaine Paulo's suggestion that Aristotle's account of contemplative activity in X.7–8 is to some extent a caricature of philosophic activity, although we offer different assessments of both the nature and purpose of this caricature. I disagree with her contention that these arguments are essentially ironic, although Paulo's analysis opens up the interesting possibility that Aristotle's use of rhetoric in the *Ethics* is also shaped by a concern for his philosophic audience, particularly those influenced by the teachings of Plato. "The Problematic Relation between Practical Virtue and Theoretical Virtue in the *Nicomachean Ethics*: Integration or Divergence?" Presented at the annual meeting of the Midwest Political Science Association, Chicago, 1994.

8. Although the peak moral virtues of magnificence and magnanimity require an abundance of resources, both material and political, Aristotle includes less splendid and less political versions of these dispositions in his account of moral virtue. Generosity and a nameless virtue regarding honor require only modest resources (see esp., 4.4.1125b1–8). Whereas the former two virtues may prove to be a hindrance to contemplation, this is not clearly the case with respect to the latter.

9. If the preceding section sketches the extent of my agreement with Hardie, Clark, and Kraut, the discussion that follows indicates something of my appreciation for the problems raised by Ackrill and Cooper.

10. Gauthier and Jolif, *L'Éthique*, vol. 2, pp. 843–44. Cf. Burnet, *Ethics*, pp. 437–38.

11. Some indication of Aristotle's restraint on this point emerges in contrast to Plato's more grating formulation of the problem in the *Republic*. Socrates likens philosophic activity to dwelling among the Isles of the Blessed, in comparison to which a preoccupation with life in the polis seems to be a kind of madness (*Rep.* 496a–e).

12. I have been influenced by Nagel's formulation of the competition between theoretical and practical reason although we emphasize different aspects of the contest. "Aristotle on *Eudaimonia*," pp. 257–58.

# BIBLIOGRAPHY OF CITED WORKS

References to Aristotle and Plato are to the page and line numbers of the Oxford Classical Text editions.

Ackrill, J. L. "Aristotle on *Eudaimonia.*" In *Essays on Aristotle's Ethics*, edited by A. Rorty. Berkeley: University of California Press, 1980.

Alpern, Kenneth. "Aristotle on the Friendships of Utility and Pleasure." *Journal of the History of Philosophy* 21 (1983): 303–15.

Ambler, Wayne. "Aristotle's Understanding of the Naturalness of the City." *Review of Politics* 47 (1985): 163–85.

Annas, Julia. "Self-Love in Aristotle." *The Southern Journal of Philosophy* 27 (1988): 1–18.

Anton, John P., and Anthony Preus, eds. *Essays in Ancient Greek Philosophy.* Vol. 2. Albany: State University of New York Press, 1984.

———, eds. *Essays in Ancient Greek Philosophy.* Vol. 4, *Aristotle's Ethics*. Albany: State University of New York Press, 1991.

Arendt, Hannah. *The Human Condition.* Chicago: Chicago University Press, 1958.

Arnhart, Larry. *Aristotle on Political Reasoning.* DeKalb: Northern Illinois University Press, 1981.

———. "Statesmanship as Magnanimity: Classical, Christian and Modern." *Polity* 16 (1983): 263–83.

Arthur, Marilyn B. "Review Essay: Classics." *Signs* 2 (1976): 382–404.

Barker, Ernest. *The Politics of Aristotle.* London: Oxford University Press, 1946.

Barnes, Jonathan. "Aristotle and the Methods of Ethics." *Revue Internationale de Philosophie* 34 (1980): 490–511.

———, ed. *The Complete Works of Aristotle.* Numerous translators. Princeton, N.J.: Princeton University Press, 1984.

Barnes, Jonathan, Malcolm Schofield, and Richard Sorabji, eds. *Articles on Aristotle*. Vol. 2, *Ethics and Politics*. New York: St. Martin's Press, 1978.

Bodéüs, Richard. *The Political Dimensions of Aristotle's Ethics*. Translated by Jan Edward Garrett. Albany: State University of New York Press, 1993.

Burger, Ronna. "Ethical Reflection and Righteous Indignation: *Nemesis* in the *Nicomachean Ethics*." In *Essays in Ancient Greek Philosophy*, Vol. 4, *Aristotle's Ethics*, edited by Anton and Preus. Albany: State University of New York Press, 1991.

Burnet, John, ed. *The Ethics of Aristotle*. London: Methuen, 1900.

Clark, Stephen. *Aristotle's Man: Speculations Upon Aristotelian Anthropology*. Oxford: Clarendon Press, 1975.

Cooper, John. "Contemplation and Happiness: A Reconsideration." In *Moral Philosophy: Historical and Contemporary Essays*, edited by Starr and Taylor. Milwaukee: Marquette University Press, 1989.

———. "Forms of Friendship." *Review of Metaphysics* 30 (1977): 619–48.

———. *Reason and Human Good in Aristotle*. Cambridge: Harvard University Press, 1975. Reprint, Indianapolis: Hackett Publishing Company, 1986.

De Croix, G. E. M. *The Origins of the Peloponnesian War*. London: Duckworth, 1972.

Defourny, Pierre. "Contemplation in Aristotle's Ethics." In *Articles on Aristotle*. Vol. 2, *Ethics and Politics*, edited by Barnes, Schofield, and Sorabji. New York: St. Martin's Press, 1978.

Dirlmeier, F. *Aristoteles: Nikomachische Ethik*. 1956. Reprint, Berlin: Akademie Verlag, 1979.

Dover, K. J. *Greek Popular Morality in the Time of Plato and Aristotle*. Berkeley: University of California Press, 1974. Reprint, Hackett Inc., 1994.

Faulkner, Robert. "Spontaneity, Justice, and Coercion: On *Nicomachean Ethics* Books III and V." In *Nomos*. Vol. 14, *Coercion*, edited by Pennock and Chapman. Chicago: Aldine/Atherton Press, 1972.

Festugière, A. J. *Aristotle: Le Plaisir*. 1936. Reprint, Paris: Librairie Philosophique, 1960.

Fortenbaugh, W. W. "Aristotle's Analysis of Friendship: Function and Analogy, Resemblance, and Focal Meaning." *Phronesis* 20 (1975): 51–62.

Gauthier, Réné. *Magnanimité: L'Idéal de la Grandeur dans la Philosophie Païenne et dans la Théologie Chrétienne.* Paris: Librairie Philosophique J. Vrin, 1951.

Gauthier, Réné, and Jean Jolif, eds. *L'Éthique à Nicomaque.* 2 vols. Louvain: Publications Universitaires, 1970.

Hardie, W. F. R. "Aristotle on the Best Life for a Man." *Philosophy* 54 (1979): 35–50.

———. "Aristotle's Doctrine That Virtue Is a Mean." In *Articles on Aristotle.* Vol. 2, *Ethics and Politics,* edited by Barnes, Schofield, and Sorabji. New York: St. Martin's Press, 1978.

———. *Aristotle's Ethical Theory.* Oxford: Clarendon Press, 1968.

———. "The Final Good in Aristotle's *Ethics.*" *Philosophy* 40 (1965): 277–95.

———. "Magnanimity in Aristotle's *Ethics.*" *Phronesis* 23 (1978): 63–79.

Irwin, Terence. *Aristotle's First Principles.* Oxford: Oxford University, 1988.

———, trans. *Nicomachean Ethics.* Indianapolis: Hackett Publishing Company, 1985.

Jaeger, Werner. *Aristotle: Fundamentals of His Development.* Translated by Richard Robinson. Oxford: Clarendon Press, 1948.

———. "Aristotle's Use of Medicine as Model of Method in His *Ethics.*" *Journal of Hellenic Studies* 77–78 (1957–58): 54–61.

Jaffa, Harry. *Aristotelianism and Thomism: A Study of the Commentary by Thomas Aquinas on the <u>Nicomachean Ethics</u>.* Chicago: Chicago University Press, 1952. Reprint, Greenwood Press, 1979.

Joachim, H. H. *Aristotle: The <u>Nicomachean Ethics</u>.* Edited by D. A. Raes. London: Clarendon Press, 1951.

Kahn, Charles. "Aristotle and Altruism." *Mind* 40 (1981): 20–40.

Keyt, David. "Intellectualism in Aristotle." In *Essays in Ancient Greek Philosophy.* Vol. 2, edited by Anton and Preus. Albany: State University of New York Press, 1984.

Kraut, Richard. *Aristotle on the Human Good.* Princeton, N.J.: Princeton University Press, 1989.

Lieberg, Godo. *Die Lehre von der Lust in den Ethiken des Aristoteles.* München: C. H. Beck'she, 1958.

Lord, Carnes. *Education and Culture in the Political Thought of Aristotle.* Ithaca, N.Y.: Cornell University, 1982.

———. "The Intention of Aristotle's *Rhetoric.*" *Hermes: Zeitschrift fur classische Philologie* 109 (1981): 326–39.

———, trans. *Politics.* Chicago: University of Chicago Press, 1984.

Lord, Carnes, and David K. O'Connor, eds. *Essays on the Foundations of Aristotelian Political Science.* Berkeley: University of California Press, 1991.

MacIntyre, Alasdair. *After Virtue.* Notre Dame: University of Notre Dame Press, 1984.

———. *A Short History of Ethics.* New York: Macmillan Inc., 1966.

Mara, Gerald. "The Role of Philosophy in Aristotle's Political Science." *Polity* 19 (1987): 375–401.

Millgram, Elijah. "Aristotle on Making Other Selves." *Canadian Journal of Philosophy* 17 (1987): 361–76.

Moravcsik, J. M. E., ed. *Aristotle: A Collection of Critical Essays.* Garden City: Doubleday & Company, Inc., 1967.

Nagel, Thomas. "Aristotle on *Eudaimonia.*" In *Essays on Aristotle's Ethics,* edited by A. Rorty. Berkeley: University of California Press, 1980.

———. "Aristotle on *Eudaimonia.*" *Phronesis* 17 (1972): 252–59.

Nichols, Mary. "Aristotle's Defense of Rhetoric." *Journal of Politics* 49 (1987): 657–77.

———. *Citizens and Statesmen: A Study of Aristotle's* <u>Politics</u>. Savage, Maryland: Rowman & Littlefield, 1992.

Nussbaum, Martha. *The Fragility of Goodness: Luck and Ethics in Greek Tragedy and Philosophy.* Cambridge: Cambridge University, 1986.

Ober, Josiah. *Mass and Elite in Democratic Athens: Rhetoric, Ideology, and the Power of the People.* Princeton, N.J.: Princeton University Press, 1989.

O'Brien, Michael. "The Unity of the *Laches.*" *Yale Classical Studies* 18 (1963): 137–47.

O'Connor, David K. "The Aetiology of Justice." In *Essays on the Foundations of Aristotelian Political Science,* edited by Lord and O'Connor. Berkeley: University of California Press, 1991.

Owen, G. E. L. "Aristotelian Pleasures." In *Articles on Aristotle.* Vol. 2, *Ethics and Politics,* edited by Barnes, Schofield, and Sorabji. New York: St. Martin's Press, 1978.

———. "Tithenai ta Phainomena." In *Aristotle: A Collection of Critical Essays*, edited by Moravcsik. Garden City: Doubleday & Company, Inc., 1967.

Pakaluk, Michael. "Friendship and the Comparison of Goods." *Phronesis* 37 (1992): 111- 130.

Paulo, Germaine. "The Problematic Relation between Practical Virtue and Theoretical Virtue in the *Nicomachean Ethics*: Integration or Divergence?" Paper presented at the annual meeting of the Midwest Political Science Association, Chicago, 1994.

Pennock, Roland, and John W. Chapman, eds. *Nomos*. Vol. 14, *Coercion*. Chicago: Aldine/Atherton Press, 1972.

Price, A. W. *Love and Friendship in Plato and Aristotle*. Oxford: Clarendon Press, 1989.

Prichard, H. A. "The Meaning of *Agathon* in the *Ethics* of Aristotle." In *Aristotle: A Collection of Critical Essays*, edited by Moravcsik. Garden City: Doubleday & Company, Inc., 1967.

Rackham, Horace, trans. *Nicomachean Ethics*. Cambridge, Mass.: Loeb Classical Library, 1956.

Rahe, Paul. *Republics Ancient and Modern*. Vol. 1, *The Ancien Régime in Classical Greece*. Chapel Hill: University of North Carolina, 1994.

Randall, John. *Aristotle*. New York: Columbia University Press, 1960.

Reeve, C. D. C. *Practices of Reason: Aristotle's Nicomachean Ethics*. Oxford: Clarendon Press, 1992.

Robinson, Robert. "Aristotle on Akrasia." In *Articles on Aristotle*. Vol. 2, *Ethics and Politics*, edited by Barnes, Schofield, and Sorabji. New York: St. Martin's Press, 1978.

Rodier, Georges. *Études de Philosophie Grecque*. Paris: Librairie Philosophique J. Vrin, 1957.

Rorty, Amélie Oksenberg. "Akrasia and Pleasure." In *Essays on Aristotle's Ethics*, edited by A. Rorty. Berkeley: University of California Press, 1980.

———. "The Place of Contemplation in Aristotle's *Nicomachean Ethics*." In *Essays on Aristotle's Ethics*, edited by A. Rorty. Berkeley: University of California Press, 1980.

———, ed. *Essays on Aristotle's Ethics*. Berkeley: University of California Press, 1980.

Salkever, Stephen. *Finding the Mean: Theory and Practice in Aristotelian Political Philosophy.* Princeton, N.J.: Princeton University Press, 1990.

———. "Women, Soldiers, Citizens: Plato and Aristotle on the Politics of Virility." In *Essays on the Foundations of Aristotelian Political Science,* edited by Lord and O'Connor. Berkeley: University of California Press, 1991.

Sherman, Nancy. "Aristotle on Friendship and the Shared Life." *Philosophy and Phenomenological Research* 48 (1987): 589–613.

Sorabji, Richard. "Aristotle on the Role of Intellect in Virtue." In *Essays on Aristotle's Ethics,* edited by A. Rorty. Berkeley: University of California Press, 1980.

Starr, William, and Richard Taylor, eds. *Moral Philosopy: Historical and Contemporary Essays.* Milwaukee: Marquette University Press, 1989.

Strauss, Leo. *The City and Man.* Chicago: Chicago University Press, 1964. Reprint, Midway, 1977.

———. *Natural Right and History.* Chicago: Chicago University Press, 1953.

Swanson, Judith. *The Public and the Private in Aristotle's Political Philosophy.* Ithaca, N.Y.: Cornell University Press, 1992.

Tessitore, Aristide. "Aristotle's Political Presentation of Socrates in the *Nicomachean Ethics*." *Interpretation* 16 (1988): 3–22.

———. "Courage and Comedy in Plato's *Laches*." *The Journal of Politics* 56 (1994): 115–33.

Urmson, J. O. *Aristotle's Ethics.* Oxford: Basil Blackwell, 1988.

Wallach, John. "Contemporary Aristotelianism." *Political Theory* 20 (1992): 613–41.

Walsh, James. *Aristotle's Conception of Moral Weakness.* New York: Columbia University Press, 1963.

Wiggins, David. "Deliberation and Practical Reason." In *Essays on Aristotle's Ethics,* edited by A. Rorty. Berkeley: University of California Press, 1980.

Wilkes, Kathleen. "The Good Man and the Good for Man in Aristotle's Ethics." *Mind* 87 (1978): 553–71.

Wilson, James Q. *The Moral Sense.* New York: Macmillan Inc., 1993.

Yack, Bernard. *The Problems of a Political Animal: Community, Justice, and Conflict in Aristotelian Political Thought.* Berkeley: University of California Press, 1993.

# INDEX

A

Achilles, 31–32, 34

Ackrill, J. L., 9, 10–11, 20, 124nn1,4, 127n25, 127–28n27, 142n9

action (*praxis*): and contemplation, 10–12; and prudence, 43; in contrast to knowledge, 13, 15–20; in contrast to philosophic inquiry, 15–20

Ajax, 31–32, 34

*akrasia*. *See* incontinence

Albert, Saint, 110

Alcibiades, 31–32, 34

Alcidamas, 116–117

Alexander of Aphrodisias, 110, 137n26

Alpern, Kenneth, 138n2

Ambler, Wayne, 139n7

Anaxagoras, 47–48, 50, 64, 109, 133n37

Annas, Julia, 140n18

appearances (*phainomena*), 52–53, 54, 135n8

*aporia* (puzzle, difficulty, problem): and friendship, 79, 83, 90; and *melancholikos*, 61–62; and pleasure, 62–64, 67; and self-love, 91; and Socratic paradox, 53, 54–57, 60–61; and theoretical foundation of the *Ethics*, 120–21; in Book VII, 52–53, 72; translation of, 134n4

architectonic art or discipline, 44, 63–65, 131n30

art (*technē*), 43; and moral virtue, 25–26

Aquinas, Thomas, 13, 110, 129n10

Arendt, Hannah, 126–27n21

Aristophanes, 2, 4, 123n4

Aristotle: as political philosopher, 50, 64, 106–107, 119–121; contrast to Plato, 107, 119-121; *De Anima*, 11; *Eudemian Ethics*, 5, 7, 17, 53–54, 62, 74, 81–82, 87, 115, 126n16, 139n11; *Magna Moralia*, 115; *Metaphysics*, 21, 67, 71, 134n4; *Politics*, 18, 33, 36, 39, 64–65, 70, 78, 80, 86, 87, 88, 108, 123n7, 126n17, 131n22, 131n28, 138n5, 141n5; *Posterior Analytics*, 31, 33, 129n11; *Problems*, 61, 70, 135–36nn15,16,17; *Rhetoric*, 4–5, 18, 126n20; *Topics*, 5

Arnhart, Larry, 4, 5, 33–34, 123nn5,6, 129n14

Arthur, Marilyn, 126–27n21

Aspasius, 137n26

B

Barker, Ernest, 136n18

Barnes, Jonathan, 126–27n21

Bodéüs, Richard, 9, 14–15, 19, 125n12

Burger, Ronna, 129n6

Burnet, John, 29, 110, 134nn4,5, 135n10, 142n10

C

character: and continence/incontinence, 57–62; and ethical virtue, 25–27; and happiness, 105; and law, 36, 41, 114; and new beginning, 51–52; and pleasure, 25–26, 60, 66, 97–102; and responsibility/voluntary, 27, 128–29n5; and rhetoric, 4–5; development of, 25–27, 46–47